# Differentiated Instruction for K–8 Math and Science:

## Activities and Lesson Plans

**Mary Hamm**
**Dennis Adams**

EYE ON EDUCATION
6 DEPOT WAY WEST, SUITE 106
LARCHMONT, NY 10538
(914) 833–0551
(914) 833–0761 fax
www.eyeoneducation.com

For information about permission to reproduce selections from this book, write: Eye On Education, Permissions Dept., Suite 106, 6 Depot Way West, Larchmont, NY 10538.

Library of Congress Cataloging-in-Publication Data

Hamm, Mary.
Differentiated instruction for K-8 math and science : activities, and lesson plans / Mary Hamm, Dennis Adams.
    p. cm.
    ISBN-13: 978-1-59667-071-6
1. Individualized instruction. 2. Cognitive styles in children. 3. Mixed ability grouping in education. 4. Mathematics—Study and teaching. 5. Science—Study and teaching. 6. Elementary school teaching. 7. Middle school teaching. I. Adams, Dennis M. II. Title.
LB1031.H35 2007
372.35—dc22

                                    2007041152

10 9 8 7 6 5 4 3 2

## Also Available from EYE ON EDUCATION

**Differentiating by Student Interest:
Strategies and Lesson Plans**
Joni Turville

**Differentiated Instruction:
A Guide for Elementary Teachers**
Amy Benjamin

**Family Reading Night**
Hutchins, Greenfeld, and Epstein

**Active Literacy Across the Curriculum:
Strategies for Reading, Writing, Speaking, and Listening**
Heidi Hayes Jacobs

**Performance-Based Learning and Assessment
in Middle School Science**
K. Michael Hibbard

**Handbook on Differentiated Instruction
for Middle and High Schools**
Sheryn Spencer Northey

**Differentiated Instruction Using Technology:
A Guide for Middle and High School Teachers**
Amy Benjamin

**The Democratic Differentiated Classroom**
Sheryn Spencer Waterman

**What Great Teachers Do Differently:
14 Things that Matter Most**
Todd Whitaker

**Seven Simple Secrets:
What the Best Teachers Know and Do**
Annette Breaux and Todd Whitaker

**Family Math Night: Math Standards in Action**
Jennifer Taylor-Cox

**Classroom Motivation From A to Z:
How to Engage Your Students in Learning**
Barbara R. Blackburn

**Teach Me—I Dare You!**
Brough, Bergmann, and Holt

# Meet the Authors

**Mary Hamm**, a former public school teacher, is currently a professor of education at San Francisco State University. She received a MA degree in environmental education from the University of Wisconsin and her doctorate is from the University of Northern Colorado. She has authored or coauthored more than ten books, and published articles in such journals as *Science and Children*, *School Science and Mathematics*, and *Educational Technology*.

**Dennis Adams** is a professor of education who works as an educational consultant in Canada. He is a former Fulbright Scholar who has done graduate work at the University of California and Harvard University. After receiving a Ph.D. in Curriculum and Instruction from the University of Wisconsin, he has written more than a dozen books and over a hundred articles. His research and writing projects have focused on topics such as language learning, technological innovation, teacher education, collaborative inquiry, and literacy for diverse populations.

# Table of Contents

# Preface

*Differentiated Instruction for K–8 Math and Science: Activities and Lesson Plans* builds on the social nature of differentiated learning to provide some practical suggestions for reaching every student in a K–8 classroom. The book is designed for teachers and prospective teachers who want ideas, activities, and lesson plans for differentiating math and science instruction. This book provides many strategies for differentiating instruction. We pay special attention to multiple intelligences because they are an important part of differentiated learning's foundation. As a teacher you'll recognize those that make sense to you and enhance your teaching. Instruction that focuses on individual interests and real-world math/science problems is more likely to motivate students.

Differentiated learning is a philosophy and a way of thinking that suggests giving careful consideration to students' learning tendencies and providing different avenues to learning and assessment. Differentiation requires a combination of teaching and assessment strategies that have positive effects on student learning. Teachers who differentiate instruction modify the content, activities, or ways individuals or small clusters of students can demonstrate and extend what they have learned. They also make sure that all learners gain an understanding of similar sets of skills or concepts. In the differentiated classroom, assessment tools and learning experiences are natural partners. Because motivation to learn often stems from the connection between authentic assessment and teaching, we focus on performance assessment, selected response, essay, communication, and portfolios that have a valued place in teaching and learning.

*Differentiated Instruction for K–8 Math and Science* is designed to help teachers create a more differentiated classroom that is open to all students. It offers a differentiated approach based on research and determined by the standards. Attention is focused on teaching methods, organizational approaches, student activities, and lesson plans designed for involving students in quality mathematics and science. Assessment is viewed as ongoing and diagnostic. The overall goal of the book is to open some exceptional doors to differentiated math and science instruction so that teachers can provide more opportunities for all learners to construct their own knowledge.

Differentiated instruction has proven helpful for teachers who want to organize math and science instruction in a way that appeals to students with different ability levels. Skilled teachers know that individual learners need to approach learning math and science in many ways. Some students think they just don't like math and science, others believe they can't be successful in these subjects. This book hopes to provide individual teachers with the differentiated learning-related tools necessary to improve attitudes and academically motivate even the most reluctant learners.

Now, more than ever, teachers are faced with reaching out effectively to students who span the entire spectrum of learning. Student differences include issues surrounding preparedness, personal interests, and cultural ways of seeing and experiencing the world. As teachers, we build on our students' strengths and work around and through weaknesses. It may take time, but good teachers often work wonders with their students. Although there is no single formula for creating a successful differentiated classroom, *Differentiated Instruction for K–8 Math and Science* presents field-tested combinations of differentiated learning with mathematical problem solving and scientific inquiry. It is hoped that this approach to differentiating learning helps teachers build on the social nature of learning and appeal to the various rates of learning found within a diverse student body.

*Differentiated Instruction for K–8 Math and Science* is written in a teacher-friendly style that helps with classroom organization and lesson planning. Although it is intended for individual teachers, the book is organized in a way that is convenient for school districts that are doing in-service work with elementary and middle school teachers. In addition to helping practicing teachers, it could also serve as a supplementary text for methods classes in mathematics and science education. The hope is for the teaching ideas, activities, and lesson plans presented here to assist teachers as they invite learners to inquire, discover concepts, and collaboratively explore the interlinking concepts of math and science.

Developing positive attitudes toward math and science goes hand-in-hand with developing competency. The biggest challenge, many teachers say, is trying to engage students and persuade them that these subjects matter. Along the way to competency, teachers can shine some light on processes involved and give everyone involved more control over the technological products of math and/or science. By demystifying practice in these areas of study, teachers can help all of their students gain a better understanding of mathematics and science.

*Differentiated Instruction for K–8 Math and Science* takes all of these issues into account when it provides differentiated math and science methods and goes on to connect them to recent pedagogical approaches that reach across the curriculum. The book builds on the expanding knowledge of what works in classrooms and suggests ways that differentiated learning can help transform mathematics and science instruction. A major goal is to support more success for more students by helping teachers develop lessons for reaching the different levels of math and science competency within their classes. Along with providing some up-to-date lesson plans for teachers, we hope to deepen the collective conversation and help teachers reverse the steady erosion of math and science skills in the general population.

# 1
# Differentiating Instruction: Introducing Different Paths to Learning

What is your largest challenge as a teacher today? Most teachers would say they are attempting to meet the broad needs, backgrounds, and learning styles of a diverse student population. Today, we know much more about why some students have little trouble learning and others struggle. We know the value of a student's preparedness, learning style, interests, and their confidence in learning.

As schools adapt to an increasingly broad range of learners, it is more important than ever to design math and science instruction in ways that accommodate academically diverse learners. Differentiated instruction (DI) can be part of the answer. With a standards-based curriculum in place in almost every state, students are expected to achieve at high levels. In the past there was a group of students who ended up placed in low-achieving classes. Now, we must find ways to make higher achievement available for everyone. Differentiated instruction is a collection of approaches that respond to the variety of learning needs in your classroom. How you effectively identify your students' learning needs and how you offer learning opportunities that increase the probability of student success characterize what differentiated instruction is all about.

Differentiated instruction is a proven way to ensure that fewer children are left behind and higher learning levels are achieved. Teachers have always dealt with the fact that individual students learn things in different ways. And most teachers realize that schools are places where they learn from students and students can learn from each other. Although differentiated math and science instruction is a more recent development, it is an easy fit for many teachers.

Differentiated instruction is nothing new. It is based on the best practices in education. It puts students at the center of learning. It allows their learning needs to drive instructional planning. The first step in differentiated learning is to begin where you are. Differentiation does not mean throwing out your planning from past years. It means analyzing how well you're providing variety and challenge in learning, recognizing which students are best served by your current plans and altering those plans as needed so more students can be successful.

# Differentiated Learning Goals

Differentiated instruction increases learning for all students by involving them in activities that respond to their individual needs, strengths, and inclinations. Some of the goals of differentiated instruction are:

- To develop challenging and engaging tasks for every learner.
- To create instructional activities based on the necessary topics, concepts, and skills of the subject, and provide ways for students to display what they have learned.
- To offer flexible approaches to content and instruction.
- To pay attention to students' readiness, instructional needs, and learning preferences.
- To meet curriculum standards for each learner (Tomlinson, 1999; Heacox, 2002).

Differentiated instruction involves tailoring instruction to meet the needs of students with a wide range of needs and academic abilities. It involves recognizing the fact that individuals and small clusters of students can use different content, processes, and products to achieve the same conceptual understanding. Differentiated responses from the teacher can be as simple as rephrasing a question—or as complicated as regrouping on the basis of student interests. Differentiated instruction is much more than individualized learning or designing a lesson for every student. It involves building mixed-ability group instruction around the idea that individual students (or groups of students) learn in unique ways and at varying levels of difficulty. Assessment can follow a similar path. And along with teacher observation, it can influence grouping decisions.

A good way for learning groups to connect with differentiated instruction is for teachers to base group assignments on what they know about the interests and aptitudes of the students involved. In addition, there are times when students may need multiple chances to demonstrate mastery. In a differentiated classroom, you will find students doing more thinking for themselves *and* working more with peers. Self-evaluation and a supportive peer assessment are part of the process. With differentiated instruction, small collaborative groups within the class are often working at different levels of complexity and at different rates. Math and science lessons can be differentiated based on a students' interest in these subjects, readiness to learn a concept, and their preferred path to comprehension.

Differentiated instruction is most effective when math and science concepts are taught in context and related to relevant prior knowledge. Differentiated instruction can provide multiple paths to understanding and expressing what has been learned. The process involves having learners construct meaning by working with peers to explore issues, problems, and solutions. In this way, DI is different from individualized instruction in that it moves beyond the specific needs and skills of each student to address the needs of clusters of students.

## How Teachers Can Differentiate or Modify Instruction

The *content* that teachers teach and how students have access to information are important ways for teachers to differentiate instruction. Curriculum content is often determined by the school or district and reflects state or national standards.

You differentiate content by preassessing students' skills and knowledge, then matching students with activities according to their readiness. Student readiness is the current knowledge, understanding, and skill level of a student. Readiness does not mean student ability; rather, it reflects what a student knows, understands, and is able to do.

*Interest* is another way to differentiate learning. Topics students enjoy learning about, thinking about, and doing provide a motivating link. Successful teachers incorporate required content to students' interests to engage the learner. This helps students connect with new information by making it appealing, relevant, and worthwhile.

A student's *learning profile* is influenced by an individual's preferred learning style, *intelligence* preference, academic interests, and cultural background. By tapping into a student's learning profile, teachers can extend the ways students learn best.

A *differentiated learning environment* enables teachers and students work to benefit each student and the class as a whole. A flexible environment allows students to make decisions about how to make the classroom surroundings work. This gives students a feeling of ownership and a sense of responsibility. Students of any age can work successfully as long as they know what's expected and are held to high standards of performance.

> To differentiate instruction, you need to clarify *the content* (what you want students to know and be able to do), *the process* (how students are going to go about learning the content), and *the product* (how they show what they know).
>
> —Amy Benjamin

# Principles of Differentiation

There are several important principles that explain a differentiated classroom. A few of them are described here:

- *A high-quality engaging curriculum* is the primary principle. Your first job as a teacher is to guarantee that the curriculum is consistent, inviting, important, and thoughtful.

- Students' work should be appealing, inviting, thought provoking, and stimulating. *Every student should find his or her work interesting and powerful.*

- Teachers should try to *assign challenging tasks* that are a little too difficult for the student. Be sure there is a support system to assist students' success at a level they never thought possible.

- *Use adjustable grouping.* It is important to plan times for groups of students to work together as well as times for students to work independently. Provide teacher-choice and student-choice groups.

- *Assessment is an ongoing process.* Teachers often preassess students to determine students' knowledge and skills based on their needs. Once you are aware of what students already know and what they need to learn, you can differentiate instruction to match the needs of each student.

- When it comes to planning activities or assignments, we often use a *tiered approach.* Tiered methods are differentiated learning ways to teach that you develop based on your diagnosis of students' needs. When you use a tiered approach, you are prescribing individual techniques to particular groups of students. Within each group, you decide whether students do assignments alone, with a partner, or as a collaborative learning team. The basic idea is to have a wide range of students learn the concept being taught. But students can reach competency in unique ways. The first step is to identify the key skills and concepts that everyone must understand. All students in a class cover the same topic, but the teacher varies materials based on student aptitudes and interests.

- *At least some grades should be based on growth.* A struggling student who persists and doesn't see progress will likely become frustrated if grade-level benchmarks remain out of his or her reach and growth doesn't seem to count. It is your job to support the student by making sure that (one way or another) they master the concepts required. When it's time for final assessments, it's helpful to plan several assessment strategies such as a quiz and a project.

# Multiple Intelligences:
# A Structure of Differentiated Instruction

The goal of differentiated instruction is to increase the chances that students are successful learners. One way to achieve this is to get to know them and to understand how they differ in interests, learning preferences, readiness, and motivation. It is important for teachers to realize that students learn and create in different ways. Although it is often best to teach to a student's strength, we know that providing young people with deep learning experiences in different domains can enrich their *intelligence* in specific areas. Tomlinson's idea of the differentiated classroom is based, in part, on the work of Howard Gardner and Robert Sternberg. They contributed to the awareness that students exhibit different intelligence preferences. Howard Gardner projected that intelligence could be thought of as a variety of independent intelligences rather than an overall measure of mental ability. He has identified eight intelligences that represent different ways a child may understand or explain their knowledge:

1. *Linguistic*: the ability to use language to express ideas
2. *Logical/mathematical*: the ability to explore patterns and relationships by manipulating objects or symbols in an orderly manner
3. *Musical*: the capacity to think in music; the ability to perform, compose, or enjoy a musical piece
4. *Spatial*: the ability to understand and mentally manipulate a form or object in a visual or spatial display
5. *Bodily-kinesthetic*: the ability to move your body through space; use motor skills in sports, performing arts, or art productions (particularly dance or acting)
6. *Interpersonal*: the ability to work in groups; interacting, sharing, leading, following, and reaching out to others
7. *Intrapersonal*: the ability to understand your inner feelings, dreams, and ideas; involves introspection, meditation, reflection, and self-assessment
8. *Naturalist*: the ability to discriminate among living things (plants, animals) as well as a sensitivity to the natural world

Sternberg suggests three intelligence preferences:

- *Analytic*: schoolhouse intelligence
- *Creative*: imaginative intelligence
- *Practical*: contextual, street-smart intelligence

Although there is still discussion about what these intelligences represent, or if there are additional intelligences, our purpose is to develop a broad collection of instructional activities that offer learning choices for each of the intelligences.

Howard Gardner added five additional abilities that control quality of information in the years ahead:

1. *Mastery of important disciplines* like mathematics, science, history, and at least one professional skill
2. *The ability to put together ideas from different disciplines* and communicate that integration to others
3. *The capacity to find out and explain new problems*
4. *Being aware of and appreciating the differences among people*
5. *Fulfilling your responsibilities as a worker and a citizen* (Gardner, 2006)

We encourage you to use these intelligences and capacities as paths for learning. Students have a range of strengths and weaknesses, and the effective teacher can put into action lessons that provide learning activities that speak to a wide assortment of these intelligences. This process ensures the best learning opportunities for students who have different strengths in each type of intelligence. Teachers are encouraged to plan their lesson activities with these intelligences in mind. For example, during a lesson on rocks, a teacher has activities that involve different intelligences.

Gardner's work can help you add excitement to the ways you teach and the projects you assign. It can also help you find out more about your students, how they learn best, and what they like to do. The activities in this book look at student actions using differentiated instruction. We explain what differentiation would look like and sound like in the classroom.

## Activities That Demonstrate Multiple Intelligence Theory

- ♦ Upper elementary and middle school students can comprehend multiple intelligence (MI) theory. One way to discover students' interests and strengths is to explain MI theory to them and provide them with a list of possible activities.

- ♦ Ask your students to review the MI activities list and note which had the most underlined. Make sure your students understand the purpose of this activity is to find out students' learning strengths.

### Student Actions

*Read the lists and underline all the MI activities that you enjoy doing, presenting, or performing. Here are some possibilities:*

**Linguistic Intelligence**

Writing an article
Developing a newscast
Making a plan, describing a procedure
Writing a letter
Writing a play
Interpreting a text or a piece of writing
Conducting an interview
Debating

**Musical Intelligence**

Singing a rap song
Giving a musical presentation
Explaining music similarities
Making up a tune
Demonstrating rhythmic patterns
Performing music

**Logical-Mathematical Intelligence**

Designing and conducting an experiment
Describing patterns
Making up analogies to explain
Solving a problem
Inventing a code
designing a Web site

**Spatial Intelligence**

Illustrating, sketching
Creating a slide show
Creating a chart, map, or graph
Create a piece of art
Drawing, painting
Videotaping

**Bodily-Kinesthetic Intelligence**

Using creative movement
Designing task or puzzle cards
Building or constructing something
Bringing materials to demonstrate
Consoling others
Using the body to persuade or support others

**Interpersonal Intelligence**

Participating in a service project
Conducting a meeting
Teaching someone
Using technology to explain
Advising a friend or fictional character

*Naturalist Intelligence*

Preparing an observation notebook
Describing changes in the environment
Caring for pets, wildlife, gardens or parks
Using binoculars, telescopes, or microscopes
Photographing natural objects

**Intrapersonal Intelligence**

Writing a journal entry
Describing one of your values
Assessing your work
Setting and pursuing a goal
Reflecting on emotions
Dreaming

**Analytic**

Reviewing basic skills review

**Creative**

Imagining, creating

**Contextual**

Being street smart

♦ Once students have expressed their choices, have them do some activities to help them remember the intelligences. We like having each student work with a partner to create activities.

♦ Use cognitive strategies: reread for meaning, ask yourself questions, take notes, make an outline, underline important ideas, look up words you don't understand in a glossary or dictionary, and so forth.

♦ Introduce various learning styles

  • *Mastery style learner*: concrete learner, step-by -step process, learns sequentially

  • *Understanding style learner*: Focuses on ideas and abstractions and learns   through a process of questioning

  • *Self-expressive style learner*: looks for images, uses feelings and emotions

  • *Interpersonal style learner*: focuses on the concrete, prefers to learn socially, and judges learning in terms of its potential use in helping others encourage students to identify their preferred learning style and get together with their team and review learning preferences.

♦ Build on students' interests. When students do research, either individually or with a group, allow them to choose a project that appeals to them. Students should also choose the best way for communicating their understanding of the topic. In this way, students discover more about their interests, concerns, learning styles, and intelligences.

♦ Plan interesting lessons. There are many ways to plan interesting lessons. Lesson plan ideas presented here are influenced by ideas as diverse as those of John Goodlad, Madeline Hunter, and Howard Gardner.

## Lesson Planning

♦ Set the atmosphere of the lesson. Focus student attention, connect the lesson to what students have done before. Stimulate interest.

♦ Activate students' prior knowledge. Ask students what they already know about the subject under study.

♦ Clarify the learning objectives and purpose of the lesson. What are students supposed to learn? Why is it important?

♦ Provide background information: Resources such as books, journals, videos, pictures, maps, charts, teacher lectures, class discussions, or seat work may be presented.

♦ Describe procedures: What are students supposed to do? This includes examples and demonstrations as well as working directions.

♦ Check students' understanding. During the lesson, the teacher may check students' understanding and adjust the lesson if necessary. Teachers invite questions and ask for clarification. A continuous feedback process is always in place.

♦ Offer guided practice experiences where students have a chance to use the new knowledge presented under direct teacher supervision.

♦ Provide students many opportunities for independent practice where they can use their new knowledge and skills.

♦ Assess and evaluate students' work to show that students have demonstrated an understanding of important concepts.

♦ Look over the lesson plan formats included in the resources at the end of the chapter.

# A Sample Multiple Intelligence Lesson Plan

## Finding Out About Rocks

Finding out about rocks is a lesson of discovery and exploration of the earth's geology. Rocks are clues to help us discover pictures of the earth's past. Geology is like detective work. The geologist examines rocks just as a detective examines tire marks, footprints, and fingerprints. Interpreting these clues is the job of both detectives and geologists. Rocks are examples of evidence that geologists use to develop ideas about the earth.

This lesson focuses on the science standards of inquiry, life science, personal/social perspectives, and technology. The math standards of problem solving, estimation, data analysis, logic, and communication are also part of the lesson.

### Lesson Goals

This lesson introduces students to the topic of geology by providing an opportunity for finding rocks, handling, and playing with them, and relating geology to music and language arts. An additional goal is to provide a dynamic experience with some of the multiple intelligences and map out a chart of rock characteristics on construction paper.

### Objectives

At the end of this lesson, students should be able to:

♦ Use specific inquiry techniques to ask questions.

♦ Demonstrate an appreciation for outdoor space by writing about feelings, or use creative drama to act out feelings

♦ Observe and make inferences based on observations

♦ Create art and literature about geology using poetry, sketches, and painting

## Grade level: K–3

### Materials

- Paper
- Pens
- Markers

Before the lesson, find an area in the school yard for a place where your students can find at least one rock. If this is not possible, have a box of assorted rocks available for them.

## Student Actions

Sort and classify the rocks by size, color, shape, and texture:

- ◆ Form groups of two or three.
- ◆ Get a bag from your teacher for collecting rocks.
- ◆ You are to find:
  - A rock smaller than the fingernail on your little finger
  - A rock that is bigger than your fist
  - A round, smooth rock
  - A rock with many colors
  - A flat rock
  - A square rock
  - A jagged rock
- ◆ While you are collecting rocks, talk about the characteristics of your rocks.
- ◆ Observe and compare your rocks with the rocks of others.
- ◆ Pick one rock.
- ◆ Describe your rock to a partner.
- ◆ Talk about your favorite rock. Tell which rock is the largest? Which rock makes you happy? Which rock is grainy? Which is smooth?
- ◆ Next, classify your rocks by size, color, shape, and texture.

| size | color | shape | texture |
|------|-------|-------|---------|
| how long, how tall | bright, dull | looks like | feels like |

- ◆ Compare and contrast your rocks with those of other students.
- ◆ As a concluding activity, make a chart of the rocks you found.

Differentiated tasks are adjusted as the teacher interacts with small groups. Students explain their findings about their rocks, write and discuss observations, and classify the rocks according to size, color, shape, and texture.

# Lesson Activities

## Activity 1: Find Your Rock

♦ Take students outdoors to the chosen site. Tell students to find one rock. Call students together after a few minutes. Have students observe their rocks using their senses. They get to know their rock by describing it to someone else. They touch their rock. The teacher then collects the rocks.

♦ Have students form a circle so they can play a game called "Find Your Rock." Have students pass their rocks to the right, behind their backs. No one is allowed to look at the rocks. Have them continue to pass their rocks around the circle, one at a time. After several passes, have everyone in the circle change places. Explain to the group that the goal of the game is for each person to get their own rock back. Have students continue passing rocks. As they identify their rocks, they should get out of the circle. The game is over when everyone has found their rocks. Differentiated instruction takes place in this activity because each group gets an assignment to match their learning strengths or interests. Have groups explain how they found their own rocks. Encourage discussion.

## Activity 2: Rock Guided Imagery Experience

Take students on a guided adventure to explore a rock. Have students prepare for a guided imagery experience by relaxing. Guided imagery is much like a story. The teacher guides students through an imaginary journey, encouraging them to create images or mental pictures and ideas. Have students get their rocks from the last class activity. Rock guided imagery should be done in a quiet, relaxed atmosphere. Teachers may wish to dim the lights or have students rest at their desks while they read the visualization.

### Guided Fantasy: A Rock

Close your eyes and imagine that you are walking in a lush green forest along a trail. As you are walking, you notice a rock along the trail. Pick up the rock. Now, make yourself very, very tiny, so tiny that you become smaller than the rock. Imagine yourself crawling around on the rock. Use your hands and feet to hold on to the rock as you scale up its surface. Feel the rock. Is it rough or smooth? Can you climb it easily? Put your face down on the rock. What do you feel? Smell the rock. What does it smell like? Look around. What does the rock look like? What colors do you see? Is there anything unusual about your rock? Lie on your back on the rock and look at the sky. How do you feel? Talk to the rock. Ask it how it got there, ask how it feels to be a rock. What kind of problems does it have? Is there anything else you want to ask the rock or talk to the rock about? Take a few minutes to talk to the rock and listen to its answers. When you're done talking, thank the rock for allowing you to climb and rest on it. Then, carefully climb down off the rock. When you reach the ground, gradually make yourself larger until you are yourself again. When you are ready, come back to the classroom, open your eyes, and share your experience (Hassard, 1990).

**Student Actions**

To differentiate, have students discuss their fantasy and offer emotional descriptions. Language arts tasks such as speaking, writing, and acting are added as the teacher interacts with small groups. A tiered approach can also be applied. Some students may be shy about sharing their fantasy experience, others are just the opposite. It's important for you to know your students and provide alternatives. Each student should have a pleasant experience.

# Activity 3: Rock Poetry

After the guided fantasy experience, students write and share ideas about their rock. In their science journal, have students list as many observations as they can. Then, have them use their observation data to write a rock Japanese poem following these directions:

- ◆ Line 1: Identify the object.
- ◆ Line 2: Write an observation of the object.
- ◆ Line 3: Share your feeling about the object.
- ◆ Line 4: Write another observation about the object.
- ◆ Line 5: End with a synonym for the name of the object.

Have students experiment with writing poems about their rocks. Use a tiered approach by assigning students to write a rock poem using selected words that the teacher and students put up on the board. Different levels of students may use detailed observations and heartfelt emotions. Some poems may be simplistic, others very advanced. Finally, have them read their poems for the class.

# Activity 4: A Rock Song

Another part of the activity is teaching a rock song to students. Teach a small group of students the words and the melody of the song, "I've Been Working On the Earth." Include struggling students in this song process. They will become the rock song "experts":

"I've Been Working In The Earth" (sung to the tune of "I've been working on the Railroad")

I've been working in the earth, all the live long day,

I've been work in the earth, just to find some rocks.

Can't you hear the pick ax snapping? Chips bouncing to and fro,

Can't you see the rocks rising? Make the pile grow!

# Activity 5:
# Introduce Graphic Organizers

Graphic organizers help students remember information. Mind mapping or webbing shows the main idea and supporting details. To make a mind map, write an idea or concept in the middle of a sheet of paper. Draw a circle around it. Then, draw a line from the circle. Write a word or phrase to describe the concept. Draw other lines coming from the circle. Then, have students draw pictures to represent their descriptions. Students can start mapping by examining the skill section of their map. Encourage students to talk about word choices and their picture creations.

## *Assessment*

Ask students what questions they have about rocks and the earth. To differentiate write *who, what, why,* and *how* on the chalkboard. Welcome all questions. The idea is for students to come up with as many questions as they can. Students develop questions based on their interests. Students use their observations to form good questions. A tiered approach also works well. Good writers generally ask good questions. A wide assortment of student questions play a role in the products produced. Encourage students to come up with many rock questions. It doesn't have to be competitive.

# Multiple Intelligences Learning Activities

## Linguistic

Have students write a reflection about the activity of collecting rocks.

### Student Actions

- What was exciting about it?
- Did you create a rock poem that you were proud of?
- Did you write a reflection in your science journal?

## Logical-Mathematical

Look at the science skills you used.

### Student Actions

Did you measure, observe, and investigate?

## Bodily Kinesthetic

Examine your rock collection.

### Student Actions

- Did you have a large collection of rocks?
- How much do you think it weighed?
- Did you role play the guided imagery activity for your group?

## Musical

Review the rock song you learned.

### Student Actions

Can you sing the song, "I've Been Working In The Earth"?

## Visual/Spatial

Draw a map of your neighborhood and point out different rock types and formations.

### Student Actions

Show the mapping or webbing similarities and differences between the rocks in your group.

## Naturalist

Find objects of different shapes in the natural environment and bring them to class to show natural differences.

### Student Actions

- Describe the changes in the natural environment.
- What did you notice about being outdoors?
- Write about your feelings.

## Interpersonal

Self-evaluate how you work in small groups and how you might improve your group work.

### Student Actions

Teach someone in your small group about the rock experiences you've had in class.

## Intrapersonal

Close your eyes and think about the different kinds of rocks that you have seen.

### Student Actions

Evaluate your work in the rock unit.

# Evaluation

Each group writes about the lesson in their journal. Journal reflections tell what students learned about rocks and how it helps them understand such learnings about geology. Encourage students to organize their work and put it in their portfolio.

Multiple intelligence theory and DI have roles to play in math and science instruction today. Lessons can be modified to meet the needs, interests, and aptitudes of small clusters of students. Lessons that incorporate differentiated learning activities are frequently designed to reach a wide variety of *intelligences* by providing an opportunity for students to display their areas of strength in math and science. As teachers adapt their lessons to reach an increasingly broad range of learners, many find that a differentiated learning model is an effective approach for ensuring that the needs of all students in a class are met.

Differentiated instruction can make any teacher's classroom more responsive to the needs of students who struggle with math and science . Differentiated instruction is a proven path to principles that can guide instruction and point to ways teachers can modify or adapt math and science content. Students' personal interests, learning profiles, and curiosity about a specific topic or skill are major considerations in differentiated learning and related assessment strategies. Tomlinson and others suggest that developing a differentiated classroom can improve teacher/student relationships and enhance academic success. An additional note of support: Many teachers report that a side benefit of differentiating instruction is that they enjoy teaching more.

# Summary and Conclusion

The term *differentiated instruction* may be new to some teachers, but many have been using related organizational strategies, concepts, and methods for years. For example, many teachers have designed lessons that build on student strengths; and they have organized small learning groups based on the varying interests of students. So, it seems safe to say that the differentiated classroom is within the reach of any teacher.

When it comes to differentiated instruction, teachers must realize that differentiation is about grouping according to students' social, academic, interests, and emotional needs. It's not about ability grouping. Teachers need the ability to build motivating lessons for mixed ability groups. And they need to think about their craft as they practice it. Better thinking also requires paying at least some attention to connecting theory and research to practice. If students have trouble learning math and science from the way we teach, we need to use their personal resources to teach them in a way they can learn.

Differentiated instruction enables teachers to plan lessons so they can meet the needs of every student in today's diverse classrooms. It has proven to be a solid asset for teachers trying to reach students who are performing at varying levels in mathematics and science. Differentiated instruction is an organized, yet flexible, way of adjusting teaching and learning to meet students where they are and help them accomplish more academically. By creating a differentiated classroom, teachers can better help students become self-reliant and motivated learners. Clearly, it is a good way to meet both individual and group needs in the regular classroom.

Because students don't all learn at the same rate, it is important to consider the pacing of math and science instruction when figuring out the differentiated options. While building on group cooperation, you can provide different individual paths for learning math and science. By having the opportunity to collaboratively explore ideas, even unmotivated students tend to respond to appropriate challenges and enjoy learning about math and science. Flexible grouping and pacing, tiered assignments, performance assessment, and other factors associated with DI can inject some fresh energy into mathematics and science instruction.

Differentiated instruction is responsive to specific individual and small group needs—as well as class performance as a whole. Successful differentiated classrooms are full of energy, excitement, and the possibility of teaching all students no matter what learning modality they prefer. Learning math and science is a process that is different for each student. In addition to individual aptitudes, teamwork skills and having a positive attitude matter. So, it is little wonder that many educators find that DI helps move students with a variety of academic strengths in the direction of viewing education as the way to light up their future.

What children can do together today they can do alone tomorrow.

—Vygotsky

# Resources

## A Lesson Plan Format for Direct Instruction

**Topic:** _____

**Grade Level:** _____

Objective: _____

Theme and/or Motivation: _____

Materials:

- •
- •
- •

Launching the Lesson: Whole-Class Teacher Instruction:

- ♦ List the concepts, definitions, and processes to be used in instruction.
- ♦ List the directions for activities and the examples you will use.

Class/Group/Individual Activities:

- ♦ Include several harder and several simpler problems that can help students at all levels of competency learn the same concept.
- ♦ How for are you going to provide for different interests, needs, and aptitudes?

Summarize:

- ♦ How will you decide whether students have learned what you wanted?

## Lesson Plan Outline for Group Investigations

**Topic:** _____

**Grade Level:** _____

What do you want students to learn?

Why are the concepts important?

What background information do students need before starting?

Organization and Procedures:

List the materials needed:

- 
- 
- 

How are you going to get the students involved?

Lesson development, questions, and desired product:

Small group options:

Gearing up (if the lesson is too easy):

Gearing down (if the lesson is too hard):

Assessment (observations, products produced, portfolio entry, etc.):

# References

Adams, D., & Hamm, M. (1998). *Collaborative Inquiry in science, math, and technology.* Portsmouth, NH: Heinemann.

Armstrong, T. (2000). *Multiple intelligences in the classroom* (2nd ed.). Alexandria, VA: Association for Supervision and Curriculum Development.

Benjamin, A. (2003). *Differentiated instruction: A guide for elementary teachers.* Larchmont, NY: Eye on Education.

Browne, M. N., & Keeley, S. M. (2000). *Asking the right questions: A guide to critical thinking* (6th ed.). Upper Saddle River, NJ: Prentice Hall.

Costantino, P., De Lorenzo, M., & Kobrinski, E. (2006). *Developing a professional teaching portfolio: A guide for success* (2nd ed.). Boston, MA: Allyn and Bacon.

Drapeau, P. (2004). *Differentiated instruction: Making it work.* New York: Teaching Resources.

Gardner, H. (2006a). *Multiple intelligences: New Horizons.* New York: Basic Books.

Gardner, H. (2006b). *Five minds for the future.* Boston: Harvard Business School Press.

Hassard, J. (1990). *Science experiences: Cooperative learning and the teaching of science.* Menlo Park, CA: Addison-Wesley.

Jacobs, H. (Ed.). (2004). *Getting results with curriculum mapping.* Alexandria, VA: Association for Supervision and Curriculum Development.

Starr, L. (2004). *Strategy of the week.* Wallingford, CT: Education World. [This online site is a place where teachers can share ideas and lesson plans.]

Tomlinson, C., & Eidson, C. (2003). *Differentiation in practice: A resource guide for differentiating curriculum, grades 5–9.* Alexandria, VA: Association for Supervision and Curriculum Development.

Tomlinson, C. (2003). *Fulfilling the promise of the differentiated classroom: Strategies and tools for responsive teaching.* Alexandria, VA: Association for Supervision and Curriculum Development.

# 2
# Differentiated Assessment

## Guiding Performance in the Elementary and Middle School

This chapter focuses on the performance assessment possibilities of which teachers are in charge. Portfolios are given special attention. A more thorough examination of assessment and evaluation is beyond the differentiated instruction (DI)-centered domain of this book. We offer some suggestions for connecting performance assessment with investigations and problem-solving work found in the differentiated math and science classroom. The objective is to support the other assessments (like tests) that allow students to show what they know.

Differentiated assessment is a philosophy of teaching that is based on the idea that teachers ought to (at least part of the time) adapt instruction and assessment to accommodate student differences. With today's progressively more diverse student body, teachers can either teach to the middle or they can expand their instruction and reach more students. In the differentiated classroom, instruction is based on what is known about students' inclinations, needs, interests, and learning profiles. Classroom assessment can follow the same model.

Performance assessments in math and science call for a clear understanding of knowledge, skills, and comprehension in these subjects. Improving student learning is our main objective. Assessment refers to the processes and techniques that are used to collect data and acquire information about students. Evaluation is considered as having more to do with making judgments based on the information gathered in the assessment process. Definitions may differ, but there is general agreement that teachers are in the best position to put any data generated to good use.

Even in the most adaptive classroom, there are some assessment and curriculum issues that have to be attended to. Official assessment, instructional assessment, and social assessment are among the most common assessment-related chores for teachers. Official assessment includes formal grading, interpreting standardized test results, and testing for special needs placement. Instructional assessment is used to plan how and when instruction will be delivered. What materials will you use? How is the lesson progressing? What changes must be made in the planned activities?

Social assessment involves figuring out how to set up groups and enhancing communication within the classroom community.

There are times when teachers can use assessment in a way that does different things for different students; such a differentiated process can enhance learning-centered assessment. The phrases *differentiated instruction* and *performance assessment* may be fairly new to you. But teachers have long considered techniques such as rephrasing questions; providing a few extra examples; or extending the time allowed for a test, activity, or project. From regrouping a class based on students' needs to giving assignment options, some teachers have used elements of differentiated learning for a long time. When it comes to assessment in today's differentiated classroom, redoing assignments and class work for full credit is at least an occasional possibility. The basic idea behind DI is that all students, regardless of differences, should be provided with whatever it takes to reach high achievement standards.

## Student Actions

- Decrease the number of *How do I/we do it?* questions.
- Ask group members before asking the teacher if you have a problem.
- Use trial-and-error discovery learning without frustration.
- Use metaphor, simile, and allegory in speaking, writing, and thinking.
- Increase your ability to work collaboratively in cooperative groups.
- Expand your willingness to begin a task.
- Start the questioning process.
- Synthesize and combine different ideas.

# Knowing Your Students

Assessing differentiated learning begins with knowing your students' learning needs. Teachers gather information about their students by finding out what students know and what they're interested in and by looking at their learning profiles.

## Students' Academic Profile

Many teachers gather information by reviewing their students' learning histories. If available, your school's ongoing record or portfolio on each student is a good place to find out information about past performance. There you will find records of standardized tests, grades, and other performance assessments. These can give you a sense about the students' classroom strengths or limitations. You can examine the results of state assessments, look at students' learning needs or modifications, and find out what their learning style preferences are.

# Student Interest Profile

To discover what interests your students both in and out of school and how they see themselves as learners, have them answer the following questions:

## Student Actions

- What is your favorite activity or subject in school? Why? Your least favorite?

- What are the easiest subjects for you? What makes them your *best* subjects?

- What are your most difficult subjects? What makes them the hardest?

- What is your most challenging subject? What makes you think and work the hardest?

- Rate the following topics according to your interests (1 = very interested, 2 = somewhat interested, 3 = not interested):

| | | | |
|---|---|---|---|
| ☐ Drama | ☐ Video games | ☐ Animals | ☐ Playing an |
| ☐ Dance | ☐ Hiking | ☐ Exercise | instrument |
| ☐ Music | ☐ Art (drawing) | ☐ History | ☐ Internet |
| ☐ Writing | ☐ Debate | ☐ Oceans | ☐ Politics/law |
| ☐ Sports | ☐ Painting | ☐ Environment | ☐ Business |
| ☐ Computers | ☐ Reading | ☐ Science | ☐ Social studies |
| | ☐ Math games | ☐ Television | |

- What are your favorite games or sports?
- If you could learn about anything, what would you choose?
- What groups, clubs, or teams do you belong to?
- What careers are you interested in?

## Alternative Assessments

Alternative assessments are ways for students to show what they know. Written correspondence can be considered alternative assessments when they are something other than traditional essays. For example, a teacher may have students write thank you notes or invitations. In the science class, written reports might be a log about caring for a plant or a pet and keeping track of its progress. In social studies, it may mean having students write an essay on what's happening in their community. Authentic assessment is another alternative assessment. Here are some ways to recognize authentic assessment:

- Does the student's work come from a need to solve a real problem?
- Does the student's task require planning, communication, or research?
- Is the student's task unforgettable?
- Does the task have real-world connections?
- Will the task take advantage of the student's strengths?
- Will every student produce the same precise result?
- Will the task enable students to better understand their learning needs?

It is not necessary for a task to meet all these questions to be considered authentic. The important idea is that authentic assessment gives the student a sense of ownership of the learning, whereas unauthentic tasks have the feel of *doing something for the teacher*. Here are some authentic activities that students do at their own desks or in a quiet corner.

### Student Actions

- Read a book of your choice.
- Write entries in your journal.
- Keep a learning log.
- Use graphic organizers.

While studying the solar system, for example, students were given these authentic tasks:

- Do some research about the planets in our solar system. Pick out some important information about each planet.
- Does the information you found match current facts about the planets?
- Draw a model of the solar system showing where the planets are at this time of year in their orbit. Show where they will be in their orbit 3 months from now.

# Assessing What We Value

Some methods for assessing educational growth have not kept up with recent research, new subject matter standards, and the way the mathematics and science curricula have changed. Multiple choice testing, for example, just doesn't do a good job of capturing the reality of today's students. Such tests convey the idea to students that bits and pieces of information count more than deep knowledge. Conversely, assessing performance is more likely to convey the notion that reasoning, in-depth understanding, taking responsibility, and the ability to apply knowledge in new situations count more.

Howard Gardner (1997) argues for assessment practices that look directly at the performance we value, whether it's a linguistic, logical, mathematical, aesthetic, or social performance. To get at what is most valued, we suggest including diagnostic assessment of prior knowledge, teacher observations, student interviews, and self-assessment. Many states include a *variety* of assessment formats: selected response such as a multiple choice essay (short answer, prompt writing) and performance assessment (creating charts and graphs). Portfolios also contain many of these elements. To be successful on state tests, students must be familiar with *every* form of assessment. Varied assessment strategies have proven helpful to teachers as they go about creating a role for students in differentiating math and science instruction. From setting goals to sharing results with others, varied forms of assessment are a good way to link assessment directly to instruction. Within this context, varied assessment formats are encountered in the *real world*, such as when taking a written driver's test, voting, or applying for a job.

In the world outside of school where people are valued for the tasks or projects they do, their ability to work with others and their responses to difficult problems or situations are what count. To prepare students for future success, varied assessment strategies should be encouraged. Assessment of work that students produce may include portfolios, writing, group investigations, projects, interactive Web sites, class presentations, or verbal responses to open-ended questions. Whether it's a small group class presentation, journal writing, storytelling, simple observation, or portfolios, alternative assessment procedures pick up many things that students fail to show on pencil-and-paper tests.

# Portfolios:
# Collecting, Selecting, and Reflecting on Work Samples

Portfolios are a major performance assessment tool for having students select, collect, reflect, and communicate what they are doing. Clearly, having students think about the evidence they have collected and decide on what it means is a good way to increase student engagement. Portfolio evaluation includes criteria students can use to identify their *best* work, and rubrics teachers can use to judge portfolio quality. Without evaluative criteria, a portfolio is not a useful tool for gauging a student's progress.

In constructing a portfolio, students can use performance or work samples to show their efforts in class participation as they conduct experiments, solve problems, and engage in collaborative inquiry. Students represent their progress in a more authentic and meaningful manner. Teachers have found that collecting, organizing, and reflecting on student work samples organized into a portfolio nicely tie in with mathematical problem solving and active scientific inquiry. Portfolios capture a more authentic portrait of a student's thinking and serve as an excellent conferencing tool for meetings with students, parents, and supervisors. In addition to portfolios, teachers often create other performance assessment tasks: projects, exhibitions, performances, and experiments. The basic idea is that by creating opportunities for students to reveal their growth, we help them concretely understand *what* they are doing and *why* they doing it.

## How to Design Portfolios

There are many ways to go about assessing performance or constructing portfolios; much depends on how the data generated is going to be used. So, before getting started, it's best to figure out whose interests are served and what processes are measured. When it comes to portfolios, we view them as a purposeful collection of student work that can be used to describe their effort, progress, and performance in a subject. There is no harm in using them to showcase the best of what a student has achieved. But most elementary and middle school teachers get more useful information when portfolios reflect student growth over a period of time. They tell a convincing story of a student's growth in competence and understanding across subjects, grading periods, semester, or the entire school year. Like other types of authentic assessment, portfolios reflect the both products of learning *and* the cognitive processes that are used to create them.

# A Student/Teacher Plan for Portfolio Development

♦ What purpose(s) do your portfolio serve?

♦ What science or math skills are assessed by each piece of information?

♦ What content categories are included in the portfolio?

♦ Who is involved in the planning and explanation processes?

♦ How many samples are included in each area?

♦ Where are portfolios be kept and who can review them?

## The Portfolio as a Tool for Understanding

Math and science portfolios have served at least three purposes: (1) to show growth over time, (2) to provide evidence of important work, and (3) to fulfill a school district or school requirement. As far as the differentiated classroom is concerned, a portfolio can be viewed as a container of evidence about a student's skills and dispositions. More than a folder of a student's work, portfolios represent a deliberate, specific collection of an individual's important experiences, questions, and accomplishments. The items are carefully selected by the student—and sometimes the teacher—to represent a cross section of a student's creative efforts. It isn't just a compendium of the best work; items are selected on the basis of what's important to all concerned. Portfolios can be even be used as a tool in the classroom to bring students together, discuss ideas, and provide evidence of understanding. The information accumulated also assists the teacher in diagnosing learners' strengths and weaknesses. And they can help the teacher communicate with parents about a students work. For all concerned, portfolios are a powerful tool for gaining a more detailed understanding of student achievement, knowledge, and attitudes.

## Advantages of Using Portfolios

It is important that teachers examine the reasons for using portfolios. If the primary purpose is to evaluate students for the purpose of assigning grades, teachers should consider having students prepare a portfolio to submit at the end of the grading period. Other reasons for this type of portfolio include evaluating the effectiveness of our instruction and showcasing what has been accomplished by students. Portfolio assessment in math and science also bring the following benefits:

♦ Helps provide organized, authentic, and continuous information.

♦ Effectively structures learning information for communication with parents and administrators.

♦ Encourages students to claim responsibility for their learning.

- Provides teachers with information about the thinking processes used.
- Measures growth over time.

When portfolios are only used for a final evaluation, it is likely that student involvement will be minimal. They produce the required content. If the purpose is to assess ongoing work, students are more likely to participate in planning, selecting criteria, and evaluating their portfolios. This generates a feeling of pride and ownership for students.

## Linking Assessment With Instruction

Portfolios are proving useful in linking assessment with instruction at every level because they allow students and teachers to reflect on their movement throughout the learning process. They also provide a chance to look at what and how students are learning while paying attention to students' ideas and thinking processes. We do not suggest that the *pure* objectivity of more traditional testing has no place in the classroom. Rather, we must respect its limits and search for more connected measures of intellectual growth. But there is no question that when coupled with other performance measures, like projects, portfolios can make an important contribution to differentiated instruction.

### *Suggestions for Assessing Small Group Work*

- Conduct at least some classroom assessment in the context of learning teams. Teachers can assess each student's achievement within a collaborative setting.
- Provide continual feedback and assessment. Learning groups need continual informal feedback on the level of learning of each member.
- Develop a list expected behaviors:
  - Prior to the lesson _____
  - During the lesson _____
  - Following the lesson _____
- Directly involve students in giving each other suggestions. Group members can provide immediate help to maximize all group members' learning.
- Avoid all comparisons between students that are based solely on their academic ability. Such comparisons decrease student motivation and learning.
- Use a wide variety of assessment tools, so lessons become a vehicle for knowledge acquisition.

# A Sample Differentiated
# Learning Activity and Assessment Grid

## Student Actions:
## Using Direct Instruction

### Dangerous Jobs and Products:
### Building Group Collaboration

A survey in the *New York Times* listed the most dangerous jobs and products in the United States (based on yearly death statistics). Your group task is to rank order each item in order of dangerousness according to the number of deaths caused each year. Place number 1 next to the most dangerous, number 2 next to the next most dangerous, and work your way down the list. Number 15 is the least dangerous:

☐ Mountain climbing

☐ Surgery

☐ Swimming

☐ Smoking

☐ Railroads

☐ Motor vehicles

☐ Police work

☐ Pesticides

☐ Home appliances

☐ Handguns

☐ Alcohol

☐ Bicycles

☐ Nuclear power

☐ Fire fighting

*Answers*: 1. smoking; 2. alcohol; 3. motor vehicles; 4. handguns; 5. swimming; 6. surgery; 7. railroads; 8. bicycles; 9. home appliances; 10. fire fighting; 11. police work; 12. nuclear power; 13. mountain climbing; 14. vaccinations; 15. pesticides

## Group Actions

♦ Form small mixed-ability teams.

♦ Team members should do the following:

• Learn how to define and organize work processes.

• Assess the quality of the processes by recording the indicators of progress.

• Place the measures on a quality chart for evaluating effectiveness.

An important *assessment part of the activity* is an observational record that is kept by one member of the group or by the teacher. It can be arranged on a grid and may be marked during the activity. (Keep it simple so the rater can participate.)

## Group Actions Using Differentiated Instruction

♦ Work in a group of four students.

♦ Explain your group's reasoning for each choice.

♦ After all the groups are done, figure the difference between the group answers and what the experts say.

♦ Compare scores. To add a little humor, figure out which groups may be in danger and which ones are relatively safe.

### Observation Form

| Group | Explaining Concepts | Encouraging Participation | Checking Understanding | Organizing the Work |
|---|---|---|---|---|
| 1 | | | | |
| 2 | | | | |
| 3 | | | | |
| 4 | | | | |

Engaging students in a *collaborative learning model* requires you to vary the ways you organize and group students. Depending on the assignment, they may work individually, in pairs, in collaborative teams, in flexible instructional groups, or as a class. You provide a range of activities that challenges students and offers variety in the ways students learn and the ways they present their learning.

## Purposeful Assessment

At the classroom level, standardized multiple choice tests have not shown themselves to be all that helpful for teachers facing complex and multifaceted socioeducational problems. When it comes to actual teaching practice, portfolio assessment has shown itself to be more dynamic than traditional testing. And when it comes to math and science, portfolios do a better job of demonstrating proficiency and showing progress toward a preset purpose. Clearly, portfolios can be used to meet the needs of evolving definitions of competency in math and science; they allow students and teachers to create, reflect, assess, and act on material that is highly thought of by those most directly involved. This helps us all go beyond simply recognizing that a mistake was made to imagining *why*, getting feedback from others, and finding practical ways to do something about it. Another element is student involvement and self-assessment, both of which are part of any differentiated instruction/portfolio package.

## Group Actions

*Student Self-Assessment Form*

Name: _____ Date: _____

Please answer the following questions in a thoughtful and truthful way.

What science or math skills are you good at now?




Which math and science skills would you like to be better at?




What could you do to improve your work in math and science?




Have you found more than one way to solve a problem?




What do you like about your work in math and science?




What have you learned about working with others?

Although you can combine the subjects, we often choose to do one of these on math, and a later one on science. After the answers are shared with other students, their work can be edited and placed in a portfolio. Flexible teams are formed where students work at their own pace.

# Assessment, Multiple Intelligence Theory, and Lesson Planning Possibilities

There is general agreement that when teachers assess learning today, they have to do more than simply test for knowledge with objective-type formats. Now, good assessment not only measures the products of learning but also the cognitive processes used to produce them. In the differentiated classroom, math and science are assessed over time; the goal is to help the student improve. Performance, thinking, and application all matter. This all has a lot to do with cognitive and metacognitive strategies—along with the mental skills required for transferring knowledge to new contexts.

Multiple intelligences (MI) theory was developed to explain how the mind worked and how understandings were reached and applied. Ideas about educational applications came later. As Howard Gardner (1997) has frequently pointed out, his ideas about multiple paths to understanding do not imply forming groups on the basis of different intelligence scores alone. Also, they do not mean having eight or nine different entry points in every lesson plan.

One useful possibility related to MI theory is the concept of individual intelligence profiles. Assessment often consists of teacher observation, rather than test scores. Intelligences are not isolated. Some individuals, for example, may have two strong areas and other fairly weak areas. Conversely, other students may have their talents evenly spread out. Once teachers have some idea of a student's strengths, they can differentiate lessons in a way that builds on that student's strengths. Sometimes, the next step is making sure that a student works with a partner who has a different profile. At other times, common interests might influence who comes together in a group of three or four.

# Multiple Intelligences (Assessment and Planning Checklist)

*Linguistic*: The ability to understand and use the spoken word and written communication. Students use accurate language, make use of new vocabulary, and clearly state ideas. They also memorize important information and communicate their needs.

*Logical-mathematical*: The ability to understand and use logic and numerical symbols and operations. Students organize information, make connections, use a variety of problem-solving strategies, and adapt and adjust to find answers. They memorize the basic facts of mathematics and learn from mistakes.

*Musical*: The ability to understand and use concepts like rhythm, pitch, melody, and harmony. Students learn commercial jingles, listen to music, sing or hum a musical piece, move to the rhythm of a favorite musical tune, or create a rhythm. They also can provide harmony to a song, clap or snap fingers in rhythm, and compose or create a song or a rap.

*Spatial*: The ability to orient and manipulate three-dimensional space. This intelligence is called visual-spatial because the visual is usually the channel for activating and processing spatial intelligence. Students can make a diagram that shows the steps they take to arrive at an answer to a math or science problem. Encourage students to make a picture or design with something they are trying to remember. Relate concepts to graphs, Venn diagrams, and branching trees. Use guided imagery to connect to concepts.

*Bodily-kinesthetic*: The ability to coordinate physical movement. Students use: movement, action, and physical contact in their class lessons. They use manipulatives in mathematics such as base-10-blocks, Cuisenaire rods, fraction pieces, pattern blocks, and calculators.

*Naturalistic*: The ability to distinguish and categorize objects or phenomena in nature. Students respond to learning math and science in a natural setting.

## Student Actions:
## Using Direct Instruction

Estimate the number of needles on this evergreen tree in the school yard. Justify your estimate with counting strategies and calculations that verify your number.

---

*Interpersonal*: The ability to understand and interact with other people. Students show empathy and kindness for others and/or demonstrate leadership. Students participate in group situations.

*Intrapersonal*: The ability to understand and use thoughts, feelings, preferences, and interests. Students share their ideas and feelings. Students assess their work.

*Existential (a relatively new possibility)*: The ability to think about questions or phenomena beyond sensory data, such as the infinite and infinitesimal. Students can defer personal needs. Students reflect on their work.

When it comes to assessment and planning in math/science lessons, one measure of intelligence or path to learning is far from sufficient. It's important to note that doing well in math and science involves several interacting intelligences. There are times, for example, when a strong spatial intelligence might improve a students' ability to conceptualize a mathematical concept or problem. At other times logical-mathematical or linguistic intelligence is the key to success. A good math or science lesson requires students to simultaneously learn along multiple dimensions. We try to build several MI points into all of our lesson plans. Again, the basic idea is to build on a student's area of strength while collaboratively addressing areas of need.

Responsive or differentiated teaching means that the teacher is attuned to the curriculum, assessment possibilities, and the students' varied learning needs. Additionally, by encouraging students to become aware of their own strengths and weaknesses, teachers can help them tap into their tendencies and the aptitudes of others. We have found that having students collect, select, and reflect on a sample of their work (portfolios) allows them to more effectively participate in their own learning and the learning of peers. Differentiated instruction and related assessment activities build on the fact that even when small groups of students have shared goals and materials, they build on their different backgrounds and cognitive strengths. It is little wonder that many of the most memorable and rich learning experiences that students have in math and science are collaborative.

Authentic assessment has a lot to do with asking for evidence of the behaviors you want to produce. For assessment to be authentic, the form and the criteria for success must be public knowledge. Students must know what is expected and on what criteria their product will be evaluated. Success should be evaluated in ways that make sense to them. It allows students to show off what they do well. Authentic assessment should search out students' strengths and encourage integration of knowledge and skills learned from many different sources. It encourages pride and may include self and peer evaluation.

# Guidelines for
# Differentiated Learning and Assessment

## Collaborative Inquiry Model
## for Science Instruction

The National Academy of Sciences suggests five phases: (1) engage, (2) explore, (3) explain, (4) elaborate, and (5) assess.

### Engage

In the *engage* phase, students are introduced to scientific questions, ideas, or natural phenomena. At this stage, scientific inquiry might focus on things like current events, local issues, scientific demonstrations, experiences on a field trip, or a question that students will encounter in the unit. Connections are made between past and present learning experiences.

### How to Design a Collaborative Lesson and Apply a Direct Instruction Assessment Strategy

Engaging students in a *collaborative learning model* requires you to vary the ways you organize and group students. Depending on the assignment, they may work individually, in pairs, in collaborative teams in flexible instructional groups, or as a class. You provide a range of activities that challenges students and offers variety in the ways students learn and the ways they present their learning. In the *dangerous jobs and products activity* earlier in this chapter, students worked in collaborative teams to rank the list of the most dangerous jobs. They compared their scores to those of the experts. Students, then, participated in an observational record to assess the quality of their work. The activity can be tiered by having students present a detailed explanation of why they ranked the jobs and activities the way they did.

## Explore

The explore phase may involve making observations in nature, collecting data on the Internet, or carrying out investigations using laboratory equipment. At this stage, students can collaboratively explain their ideas to others. The next step is moving from the different ideas generated to build a common base of experiences and actively explore their environment or manipulate materials.

### How to Design a Tiered Lesson and Apply a Direct Instruction Assessment Strategy

The tiered model can be organized by complexity. You address the needs of students who are at the beginning levels of learning as well as those who are ready for more in-depth or advanced work. Here are three sample activities tiered by complexity:

1. *Least complex*: Create an informational booklet to inform your classmates about an environmental issue related to rain forests.

2. *More complex*: Create an informational booklet to inform your classmates of different points of view about an environmental issue related to rain forests.

3. *Most complex*: Create an informational booklet that presents various positions about an environmental issue related to rain forests. Describe your position and present a convincing argument for it. In the rain forest interdependence activity in Chapter 3, students used a tiered approach to discuss the connections that they made. This can be done at the least complex, more complex, and most complex levels.

## Explain

The purpose of the *explain* phase is to develop explanations and to get students to use some scientific terms. Along with formal language, the content can make earlier experiences easier to describe and explain. The explain phase can be linked to *learning center assessments.*

### How to Design a Learning Center Model Lesson and Apply a Direct Instruction Assessment Strategy

The learning-centered model is described in the unknown liquids experiment in Chapter 3. This learning center workshop model has student teams experimenting trying to discover what the mystery liquids are. Flexible teams are formed where students work at their own pace. They perform a variety of tests as they rotate through the five centers.

## Assessment

In the *assessment* phase, students are encouraged to assess their understandings as they apply what they learned through scientific inquiry. They can also produce evidence of how they apply concepts in their math and science portfolio or in a section of a portfolio that covers their work across the curriculum.

### How to Design a Portfolio Model and Apply a Direct Instruction Assessment Strategy

The portfolio assessment model is used in lessons throughout Chapters 3, 4, and 5. Students reflect on their work often in a science or math journal or put their assignments in a portfolio.

Thomas Aquinas looks at taking risks in the following quote. Teachers and students take risks when they design portfolios. But as he says, if your aim is to "preserve your ship," you would not create a portfolio.

> If the highest aim of a captain was to preserve his ship then he would stay in port.

> —Thomas Aquinas

# Hints for Helping
# Teachers Differentiate Learning

Nearly all educators agree with the goal of differentiated instruction, but teachers may not have strategies for making it happen. Following are a few hints that teachers can use to enhance instruction.

♦ *Assess students*: The role of assessment is to foster worthwhile learning for all students. Some assessment strategies that are helpful for students with learning problems include formal performance assessments and informal assessment tools such as rubrics, checklists, and anecdotal records. Teachers should be encouraged to assess students before beginning a unit of study or development of a skill.

*How to construct a quality rubric*: A rubric is a rating scale to be used to sort students' work into four piles.

4. Exemplary work: Goes well beyond expectations of the task-for example a problem is solved more than one way or completed a more difficult solution.

3. Excellent work: Task is completed with no errors.

2. Task is completed with only a few minor errors. Work shows understanding of the task.

1. Students who do not understand and need more instruction (student work may include evidence that the task was not understood completely; may include faulty reasoning; may make significant errors. (Reys, Lindquist, Lambdin, Smith, & Suydam, 2003).

♦ *Create complex instruction tasks.* Complex tasks are as follows:

• Open-ended

• Intrinsically interesting to students

• Uncertain (thus allowing for a variety of solutions)

• Involve real objects

• Draw on multiple intelligences in a real-world way

♦ *Incorporate television effectively into a lesson:* Use television to add information to a lesson. Television programs like Nova can reach students at their interest level.

♦ *Use materials and activities that address a wide range of reading levels, learning profiles, and student interests.* Include activities that range from simple to complex, from concrete to abstract.

♦ *Use math or science notebooks.* Math or science notebooks are an everyday part of learning. The math and science notebook is more than a record of collected data and facts of what students have learned. They are notebooks of students' questions, predictions, claims linked to evidence, conclusions, and reflections. A math and science notebook is a central place where language, data, and experiences work together to produce meaning for the students. Notebooks support differentiated learning. They are helpful when addressing the needs of disinterested students. In a science notebook, even students who may have poor writing skills can use visuals such as drawings, graphs, and charts to indicate their learning preferences. There is ongoing interaction in the notebooks. For teachers, a notebook provides a window into students' thinking and offers support for all students (Gilbert & Kotelman, 2005).

♦ *Provide clear directions for students.* Teachers need to offer instructions about what a student could do if he or she needs help.

♦ *Use a record-keeping system to monitor what students do.*

♦ *Include a plan for on-going assessment.* Teachers use ongoing assessment of student readiness, interest, and learning profile for the purpose of matching tasks to students' needs. Some students struggle with many things, others are more advanced, but most have areas of strengths. Teachers do not assume that one set of skills fits all students.

♦ *Modify a curricular element,* such as content, process, or products. We suggest doing this when you see a student in need and you are convinced that the learner will understand important ideas and skills more thoroughly as a result.

I believe that we should get away altogether from tests and correlations among tests and look instead at more naturalistic sources of information about how peoples around the world develop skills important to their way of life.

—Howard Gardner

## Resources and References

Abell, S. and Volkmann, M. (2006). *Seamless assessment in science: A guide for elementary and middle school teachers.* Portsmouth, NH: Heinemann.

Airasian, P. W. (2000). *Classroom assessment: Concepts and applications.* New York: McGraw-Hill.

Borich, G., & Tombari, M. (2004). *Educational assessment for elementary and middle school education.* Upper Saddle River, NJ: Pearson Education.

Criswell, J. (2006). Developing assessment literacy: a guide for elementary and middle school teachers. Norwood, MA: Christopher-Gordon.

Gardner, H. (1997, September). Multiple intelligences as a partner in school improvement. *Educational Leadership,* 55 (1): 20–21.

Gregory, G., & Kuzmich, L. (2004). *Data driven differentiation in the standards-based classroom.* Thousand Oaks, CA: Corwin.

McMillan, J. H. H. (2000). *Classroom assessment: Principles and practice for effective teaching.* Boston: Allyn & Bacon.

Montgomery, K. (2000). *Authentic assessment: A guide for elementary teachers.* Boston: Addison Wesley.

Nitko, A. J. (2000). *Educational assessment of students.* Upper Saddle River, NJ: Prentice Hall.

Reys, R., Lindquist, M., Lambdin, D., Smith, N., Suydam, M. (2003). *Helping children learn mathematics (6th Ed.). New York: J. Wiley & Sons.*

Salvia, J. (2001). *Assessment.* Boston: Houghton Mifflin.

Stiggins, R. J. (2000). *Student-involved classroom assessment.* Upper Saddle River, NJ: Prentice Hall.

Tomlinson, C. (1999). *The differentiated classroom: Responding to the needs of all learners.* Alexandria, VA: Association for Supervision and Curriculum Development.

Wormmeli, R. (2006). *Fair isn't always equal: Assessing and grading in the differentiated classroom.* Portland, ME: Stenhouse.

www.assessmentinst.com and www.makingstandardswork.com are two Web sites we often use to explore assessment issues and practices.

# 3

# Differentiating Mathematics Instruction

Students in our nation's schools today are more diverse than ever; they differ by abilities, interests, and preferred paths for learning math. Effective teachers know that there is potential in every student; you just have to find the key to unlock those possibilities.

Many teachers differentiate instruction, even if they don't know what to call it. Differentiated instruction (DI) is a continuous process of learning about students' needs and interests and using that information to guide instruction. By making a distinction of student work, teachers can give everyone the opportunity to move beyond basic skills to higher levels of mathematical thinking.

High-quality mathematics teaching and learning involve much more than procedures and facts. It begins with inquiry and is constructed concept by concept, question by question, and problem by problem. Here, we take that into account and examine how DI can bring the beauty of mathematics to students with very different personal backgrounds, abilities, and preferences. In the differentiated classroom, it is assumed that all students can learn math.

Over the last two decades, American mathematics instruction has received more attention and student achievement in mathematics has been growing. In 2000, the revised mathematics teaching standards were published by the National Council of Teachers of Mathematics (NCTM). It stressed the importance of the national math standards in every state and helped raise the status of mathematics instruction in the national agenda. The standards document makes it clear that students differ from one another as much in how they learn as they do in shape, size, and social development. Many teachers are familiar with the NCTM standards and often address them in their teaching.

Differentiated instruction fits into a stable math curriculum. It is especially helpful for teachers who are designing math instruction for students with many ability levels and interests. In today's schools, it is no longer possible for students to spend most of their time on computation, memorization, and routine practice activities—with a few of the more academically adept going on to advanced mathematics. Now, everyone must pay attention to computational understanding, reasoning, genuine problems, and connections among math ideas. Certainly, it is hard for students to do advanced mathematics if they are missing the most basic math skills. So, it seems safe to say that the development of advanced mathematical understanding and basic skills depend on each other.

One way that teachers teach for mathematical understanding is by building up skills and deeper concepts so that students can connect new ideas to what they already understand. We suggest beginning with a variety of DI strategies that are challenging, yet not threatening. For this to work efficiently, teachers must know their students and provide them with a nurturing environment. As teachers differentiate instruction, it becomes easier to actively build student knowledge, interaction, and problem solving on daily basis. Another common feature of a differentiated classroom is that learners are often asked to act with initiative and purpose in determining how they go about doing their work. Effective teachers make sure that everyone knows that there isn't just one way of thinking about problems. By encouraging students to consider a variety of approaches and solutions, it is easier for them to view problems in more of a real-world context.

## Differentiating the Learning of Mathematics

There are several ways teachers can differentiate or modify instruction in the math classroom. As we pointed out in Chapter 1 explaining content, connecting with students' interests, tapping into students' learning profiles, and providing a differentiated learning environment are important for effective math instruction.

Many people have their own ideas of what mathematics is. Which of the following views of mathematics is closest to yours? Here, we offer a few views and give some suggestions of how to apply them.

## Mathematics Is a Way of Thinking and Asking Questions

### Student Actions

1. List all the times outside of school where you used math this week.
2. How often did you use math today: looking at the clock, lining up in the supermarket checkout queue, buying a lunch ticket, for example?

## Mathematics Is a Knowledge of Patterns and Relationships

### Student Actions

1. Show how one math combination (like 4 + 2 = 6) is related to another basic fact (like 6 – 4 = 2).

2.  Advanced thinkers: Show how multiplication and division are interrelated $4 \times 3 = 12$ and $12 \div 3 = 4$). Have them use their observation skills to describe, classify, compare, measure, and solve problems.

3.  The advanced thinker can explain the math relationships the class has discovered by inventing a scary mystery problem either by using addition, subtraction, multiplication, or division.

# Math Is a Tool That We Use Every Day

## Student Actions

1.  Solve this problem using the tools of mathematics. A man bought an old car for $50 and sold it for $60. Then, he bought the car back for $70 and sold it again for $80. How much money did he make or lose?

2.  Do the problem with your group and explain your reasoning.

    Gearing Down

    • Have students use play money and act it out.

    Gearing Up

    • Try the problem again using a different strategy.

# Math Is Having Fun

It's similar to solving a puzzle. Math video games are exciting challenges for many elementary and middle school students, such as Amazon Football Math, Math Blaster, and Math Commander.

## Student Actions

1.  Play a math video game with your group.

    Gearing Up

    • Explain the video game.

    • Compare the game with another math game.

    • How are they alike or different?

    Gearing Down

    • Share something about the video game. What did you like?

2.  With a partner, play a game of cribbage (a card game in which the object is to form combinations for points).

    Gearing Up

    • Keep track of your points.

    Gearing Down

- Play a game of math bingo:

  The teacher calls out a number from zero to five.

  The students place that many markers on a bingo card.

  Then, the teacher calls out another number and the students place that many additional markers on their board.

  The students check their bingo cards for the total number.

## Math Is an Art

### Student Actions

- ♦ With a small group of students, design a picture.

  Gearing Down

  - Have students find shapes and label them.

  Gearing Up

  - Create a mystery or futuristic art picture using geometric shapes.
  - Label the shapes.

## Math Is a Specialized Language

It uses special terms and symbols to represent information.

### Student Actions

1. Brainstorm about favorite hobbies, television programs, kinds of pets, or favorite video games. Share with your group.
2. Once a topic is agreed on, organize and take a survey of all class members. When the data are gathered and compiled, have groups make a clear, descriptive graph that can be posted in the classroom.

   Gearing Down

   - Form a good question, such as, "What kind of pet do you own?"

   Gearing Up

   - Investigate the question, asking questions such as, "Why do most people in class own a cat or a dog?" Explain your reasoning.

## Math Is Interdisciplinary

Gearing Down

- With a group, design a song using rhythmic format that can be sung, chanted, or rapped.

Gearing Up

- The lyrics can be written and musical notation added.

# Guidelines for Differentiating Math Instruction

♦ *Less is better.* Students who are having difficulties with math problems perform better if they have fewer problems to solve. A smaller number of problems that are similar let students develop a deep understanding of how to arrive at a solution.

♦ *Describe information at three levels.* Math concepts can be presented at three levels: (1) concrete (using manipulatives), (2) pictorial (using pictures), and (3) abstract (when you explain the problem to someone else).

♦ *Focus on math patterns.* Patterns such as counting by twos, threes, fives, and tens can help students with simple multiplication math facts. Patterns can be used as helpful steps in finding solutions to problems. You can emphasize math patterns that use movement as classroom *games* at various points during the day.

♦ *Use creative methods to teach basic facts.* Teaching math combinations through the use of songs, rhythms, and other novel teaching techniques improves students' memory for learning basic math combinations. These techniques are entertaining for students and help students who learn better using their strength in musical intelligence.

♦ *Structure a lesson that focuses on students' strengths.* Use a number of intelligences to present the math information. For example, you may create a movement activity to practice math facts. Teachers often find new ways to represent the math combinations with bodily movements (touching your head, shaking your finger, stamping your feet, and so on). Such innovation improves the students' learning and provides better retention.

♦ *Use genuine situations.* Teachers often use real-world examples and make associations between students' previous knowledge and new information using actual situations. These kinds of activities motivate students to learn math as well as improve interpersonal relationships.

♦ *Recognize students' math fear.* Too many students fear mathematics because they remember their early math failures. Teachers can have students work in pairs or small groups to share their experiences and arrive at solutions together.

# Learning Mathematics With the National Council of Teachers of Mathematics Standards

The standards describe the mathematical content and processes that students should learn. They call for a larger range of mathematics studies, pointing out what should be valued in mathematics instruction. The 10 standards describe a thorough foundation of what students should know and be able to do. They affirm the understandings, knowledge, and skills required of elementary and middle school students.

All students should have the opportunity to learn important mathematics. The *Principles and Standards for School Mathematics* reinforce teachers' abilities to do that by including information about the way students acquire mathematical knowledge. The standards include content (addressing what students should learn) and process (addressing aspects of doing mathematics). The content standards: number and operations, algebra, geometry, measurement, data analysis, and probability explain the foundations of what students should know. The process standards of problem solving, reasoning and proof, communicating, making connections, and representing data communicate ways of using and applying content knowledge.

## Connecting the Curriculum Standards to School Mathematics

The next section of this chapter links the standards to classroom practice by presenting few sample activities for each standard. The purpose is not to recommend an activity for a specific grade level, but to present activities that can be used in many grades. These lessons were field tested in math classrooms in the San Francisco Bay Area.

### Standard 1: Number and Operations

Concepts and skills connected to number are a basic emphasis for beginning elementary students. Number sense invites children to make sense of what the numbers mean and compare them to actual world situations. Teachers can help students strengthen their sense of number by moving from preliminary basic counting techniques to more sophisticated understanding of numbers, when they make sense of the ways numbers are used in their everyday world.

How students acquire their *number sense*:

Stage 1.    At this entry stage, most children don't have knowledge of quantity. Students do not understand the notions of *fewer* or *greater*. However, they may be able to count and identify the number symbol. They can point to the numeral 3, but they do not know the actual meaning of the number.

Stage 2.    Students at this level start to understand number sense. A child understands and talks about words like *lots*, *five*, and *ten*. However, they do not yet understand simple computational skills; but they know greater and lesser amounts.

Stage 3.    At this level children have a beginning sense of counting. They solve problems by counting up from one. They often use their fingers or objects to solve a problem. They make many errors in counting.

Stage 4.    Children use counting up strategies or counting on. They may hold up fingers or use objects to find a solution for a problem such as 4 plus 2 more.

Stage 5.    At this stage, children have a mastery of number sense. They respond quickly and correctly when asked the answer to a problem. They have learned math facts such as 5 + 3 = 8. They can reverse the process to show 8 - 3 = 5.

## Suggestions for Teaching Number Sense

Several differentiated strategies have been suggested for developing number sense. Some are based on simple games and mathematical play for students. A few ideas are presented here:

♦ *Match numbers with objects*: Students label objects and identify the numbers that the object contains. You can encourage more advanced learners to deal with higher numbers. Rather than counting from one to ten, students count by twos to 100.

♦ *Play counting games*: Even young children can count to 10. Having the class count out loud erases embarrassment. the following text describes some examples of counting activities.

## Student Actions

### Gearing Down

1.  Count together how many books are on the bookshelf?
2.  Count the number of cushions the class needs to make a reading center.
3.  After a few days of counting, combine counting with written numbers.

### Gearing Up

Write a three-digit number where the first and third digits are different by at least 2.

### Gearing Down

1.  Count with a calculator
2.  Show how you did it.

### Gearing Up

1.  Count backwards with a calculator.
2.  Explain how to do it.

### Student Actions

1. Extend counting patterns.
2. Rather than counting 1 to 10, count from 101 to 110.
   - Use estimation strategies: Talk about estimation skills with students using terms *more than* and *less than*. Encourage students to estimate within a certain range. "I have more than four and less than eight, what number do I have?"

### Student Actions

*Gearing Down*

- Give us a number between 30 and 80.
- How many shoes went to lunch today?
- How many toes walked to the playground?
- How many of your classmates can count by threes?

*Gearing Up*

- What is greater than $5,555,000.00?
- What could I buy with all that money?

# Math Games and Differentiated Activities to Teach Number Sense

## Activity 1: Find My Mistake

Teachers can ask students to find classroom math mistakes. With this game, teachers may repeat or skip numbers while counting. Students identify the mistake and correct it. The teacher starts the counting game by having students count with him or her.

### Student Actions: Applying Direct Instruction

Teacher: "1, 2, 4, 5, 6, 7."
Students: "You missed three!"
Teacher: "10, 11, 12, 12, 13, 14, 15."

Students who are listening may quickly notice 12 was repeated. Student volunteers can continue to be the counter who makes mistakes.

Some children learn the number sequence to 20 even up to 100 without being able to count a set of objects less than 20. Some students who know the number sequence sometimes make counting errors by counting objects in a set more than once or not counting others. They do not establish a one-to-one correspondence. This rote counting session reinforces the foundation of number, comparing sets, learning the sequence of number names, and the numerals to represent numbers to help children form an understanding of number concepts (Cathcart, Pothier, Vance, & Bezuk, 2006).

# Activity 2:
# Demonstrate Math Facts

Teachers ask young students to show their understanding of math facts, such as eight is greater than five or three is less than seven. For advanced students, try a problem solving game: "I have six licorice pieces. Pretend my fingers are pieces of licorice." (The teacher holds up three fingers, while hiding one hand behind his or her back. "How many am I hiding from you?")

Actively involve students in demonstrating math problems.

## Student Actions:
## Join Problem

1. Introduce a mystery problem:
   - Joe had 3 cookies and Jenny gave him 7 more cookies. How many cookies does Joe have now?
2. Change the mystery:
   - Joe had 3 cookies and Jenny gave him more cookies. How many cookies did Jenny give Joe?
3. Start the mystery
   - Joe had some cookies and Jenny gave him 7 cookies. Now, Joe has 10 cookies. How many cookies did Joe have to start with?

## Student Actions:
## Separate Problem

4. Result mystery:
   - Joe had 10 cookies. He gave 7 cookies to Jenny. How many cookies does he have now?
5. Change the mystery:
   - Joe had 10 cookies. He gave some cookies to Jenny. Now, Joe has 3 cookies. How many cookies did he give to Jenny?
6. Start the mystery:
   - Joe had some cookies. He gave 7 cookies to Jenny. Now Joe has 3 cookies. How many cookies did Joe start with?

Have students draw a picture or write a corresponding number sentence showing each problem. In a join problem, cookies are being added or joined to a set. The three amounts involved are the starting amount, the change amount, and the

technology amidst the various disciplines, giving students the tools they need to improve society.

# The Stimulating World of Science Education

Science can be one of the most exciting experiences for elementary and middle school students and teachers if it is taught as an active hands-on subject where students learn through doing. Science provides creative teachers with many opportunities for helping to teach students who struggle with science. This has been difficult in the past. Science terms seemed nearly hopeless to understand. Many students felt science was uninteresting and boring. (Really, tedious.) How can teachers help students trudge their way through it or pass the tests? For elementary and middle school students challenged by their science textbooks, those who aren't naturally drawn to the sciences for whatever reason, and those who can't seem to connect ideas to knowledge comprehension, it is a major problem. We want these students to know they are not alone.

# Different Learning Approaches

Many strategies are based on the idea that teachers adapt instruction to student differences. Today, teachers are determined to reach all students, trying to provide the right level of challenge for students who perform below grade level, gifted students, and everyone in between. They are working to deliver instruction that meets the needs of auditory, visual, and kinesthetic learners, while trying to connect to students' personal interests. Following are some teaching strategies for differentiated instruction (DI). They are starting points for consideration, not a complete guide. Feel free to revise and edit the list as you see fit.

## Use a Collaborative Approach

Collaborative learning is an approach that lends itself to DI. It requires everyone to think, learn, and teach. Within a collaborative learning classroom, there are many and varied strengths among students. Every student possesses characteristics that lend themselves to enriching learning for all students. Sometimes these *differences* may represent a conventionally defined *disability*; sometimes it simply means the inability to do a certain life- or school-related task. And sometimes it means, as with the academically talented, being capable of work well beyond the norm. Within the collaborative learning classroom, such exceptionality need not constitute a handicap.

Collaborative learning is not simply an approach that a teacher can just select and adopt to *accommodate* a student within the classroom. Making significant change in the classroom process requires that teachers undergo changes in how they teach and how they view students. This means creating comfortable, yet challenging, learning environments rich in diversity. The goal is collaboration among all types of learners.

In mixed-ability groups, the emphasis must be on proficiency rather than on age or grade level as a basis for student progress.

Active collaboration requires a depth of planning and a redefinition of planning, testing, and classroom management. Perhaps most significantly, collaborative learning values individual abilities, talents, skills, and background knowledge.

## Form Multiage Flexible Groups

To maximize the potential of each learner, educators must meet each student at the individual's starting point and ensure substantial growth during each school term. Classrooms that respond to student differences benefit virtually all students. Being flexible in grouping students gives students many options to develop their particular strengths and show their performance.

## Set Up Learning Centers

A learning center is a space in the class that contains a group of activities or materials designed to teach, reinforce, or extend a particular concept. Centers generally focus on an important topic and use materials and activities addressing a wide range of reading levels, learning profiles, and student interests.

A teacher may create many centers such as for science, music, or reading. Students don't need to move to all of them at once to achieve competence with a topic or a set of skills. Have students rotate among the centers. Learning centers generally include activities that range from simple to complex.

Effective learning centers usually provide clear directions for students including what students should do if they complete a task or if they need help. A record-keeping system should be included to monitor what students do at the center. Also, an ongoing assessment of student growth in the class should be in place, which can lead to teacher adjustments in center tasks.

## Structure Varied Tiered Activities

There are helpful strategies available for use when teaching a student who struggles with reading from a science textbook or has a difficult time with complex vocabulary and needs some help making sense of the important ideas in a given chapter. At the same time, a student who is advanced well beyond grade level needs to find a genuine challenge in working with the same concepts.

Tiering can be focused on the challenge level, where students are challenged with complex levels of difficulty, resources, tiered by outcomes, and products. You decide on the best approach based on your learning needs.

The tiered challenge level is based on Benjamin Bloom's higher levels of thinking.

- ◆ *Knowledge* is the first level; students recall facts and learned information. Example: List the facts about gravity.

- *Comprehension* is the second level; students show their understanding with what they have learned. Having students explain or describe helps them think at the comprehension level. Example: Explain the uses that gravity has in everyday life.

- The *application* level of thinking has students demonstrate and use their knowledge. Example: Organize an activity that uses gravity.

- *Analysis* is next, when you ask students to critically examine compare, contrast, and classify your using a high level of thinking. Example: Compare and contrast what happens when you drop a rock from a high building as opposed when you drop it a few feet from the ground.

- *Evaluation* follows; students judge, predict, verify and assess. Example: What do you think would happen if your computer fell from the table while you were working? How could you justify breaking it?

- *Synthesis* comes next; students create, hypothesize, and invent. An illustration involves synthesis if it requires original thinking. For example, students can be asked to design a pencil or pen that won't fall off the table.

The first level in Bloom's taxonomy is knowledge. There are times when students need more time to work on skills and other students are more advanced. You may begin your tiering procedure by crafting a basic task from the bottom step of the ladder and then developing activities of greater challenge or difficulty.

Teachers use tiered activities so that all students focus on necessary understandings and skills but at different levels of complexity and abstractness. By keeping the focus of the activities the same, but providing different routes of access, the teacher maximizes the likelihood that each student comes away with important skills and is appropriately challenged.

Teachers select the concepts and skills that will be the focus of the activity for all learners. Using assessments to find out what the students need and creating an interesting activity that causes learners to use an important skill or understand a key idea are a part of the tiered approach. It is important to provide varying materials and activities. Teachers match a version of the task to each student based on student needs and task requirements. The goal is to match the task's degree of difficulty and the students' readiness.

## Make Learning More Challenging

Challenging strategies emphasize authentic problems more and encourage students to formulate their own problems on a topic that truly interest them, which they can explore as a team. It is best to have students pursue *real-world* problems and allow time for discussion and a sharing of ideas.

## Have a Clear Set of Standards

Integrating standards into the curriculum helps make learning more meaningful and interesting to reluctant learners. Having a clearly defined set of standards helps teachers concentrate on instruction and makes clear to students the expectations of the class. Students come to understand what is expected of them and work collaboratively to achieve their goals. Challenging collaborative groups to help each other succeed is another way to avoid poor performance.

## Expand Learning Options

Not all students learn in the same way or at the same time. Teachers can expand learning options by differentiating instruction. This means teachers reaching out to students or small groups improve their teaching to create the best learning experience possible.

## Introduce Active Reading Strategies

This approach uses *active reading* strategies to improve students' abilities to explain difficult text. This step-by step process involves reading aloud to yourself or someone else as a way to build science understanding. Although most learners self-explain without verbalizing, the active reading approach is similar to that used by anyone attempting to master new material. It has been found that the best way yet to truly learn is to teach and to explain something to someone else.

# The Changing Science Curriculum

Today, active science learning in the elementary and middle schools is changing the boring textbook process. It contributes to the development of interdisciplinary skills. For example, the overlap in mathematics and science is obvious when you look at common skills. Many of the best models in science education involve having students work in cross-subject and mixed-ability teams. Teachers begin by making connections among science, mathematics, and real-world concerns (good examples are found in newspapers). The live action of science education and literacy is in the hands of teachers.

To use and understand science today requires an awareness of what the scientific endeavor is and how it relates to our culture and our lives. Inquiry involves curiosity, observation, posing questions, and actively seeking answers.

# The National Science Content Standards

The content standards clearly articulate what students should know, understand, and be able to do:

- Understand the basic concepts and processes in science.
- Use the process of inquiry when doing science.
- Apply the properties of physical science, life science, and earth and space science when doing activity-based learning.
- Use science understandings to design solutions to problems.
- Understand the connection between science and technology.
- Examine and practice science from personal and social viewpoints.
- Identify with the history and nature of science through readings, discussions, observations, and writings. (National Research Council, 1996)

# Inquiry in the Science Standards and Process Skills

The inquiry skills of science are acquired through a questioning process. Inquiry also raises new questions and directions for examination. The findings may generate ideas and suggest connections or ways of expressing concepts and interrelationships more clearly. The process of inquiry helps students grow in content knowledge and the processes and skills of the search. It also invites unmotivated learners to explore anything that interests them. Whatever the problem, subject, or issue, any inquiry that is done with enthusiasm and with care uses some of the same thinking processes as scholars who are searching for new knowledge in their field of study.

Inquiry processes form a foundation of understanding and are components of the basic goals and standards of mathematics and science. These goals are intertwined and a multidisciplinary approach provides students many opportunities to become involved in inquiry. Each goal involves one or more processes (or investigations). The inquiry process approach includes the major process skills and standards as outlined in the activities that follow. The science activities also include the key principles of a differentiated classroom (Tomlinson, 1999).

# Science Activities
# Based On the Science Standards

This section connects the science standards to elementary and middle school classrooms. The importance of establishing activities that use the inquiry skills of observing, measuring, recording data, and drawing reasonable conclusions is emphasized. Some activities are based on concepts developed by the National Science Foundation: Science Curriculum Improvement Study and Science-A-Process Approach. Although different in detail and flavor, all depend on student investigations for learning and ultimately became known as inquiry science curriculum (Pine & Aschbacher, 2006). Whenever possible, mathematics is included in activities so that math and science skills are developed together. Careful attention has been given to the sequence of activities within each section. Some activities have originated from the AIMS Education Foundation, 1987 (AIMS Activities to Integrate Mathematics and Science). The differentiated lesson modification suggestions were field tested by students at San Francisco State University. The more general introductory activities come first, followed by more focused activities that build on each other to develop student understanding. At the end of each activity, suggestions for DI are offered. These ideas provide *a peek* into the differentiated process so that teachers can try out some differentiated strategies with their students.

# Science Activities

## Activity 1:
## Buttons and Shells (Grades K–5) (AIMS)

### Inquiry Skills

Observing, classifying, comparing, sequencing, solving problems, group work, communicating, recording, gathering data, measuring.

### Science Standards

Inquiry, physical science, science and technology, personal perspectives, written communications.

### Description

In this introductory activity, students are observing by looking at the details of an object closely. Students collect evidence by classifying, comparing, sequencing, gathering data, and trying to solve problems. Students communicate and work in groups to arrive at a solution.

### *New Vocabulary*

Sorting, seriation, gradation, Venn diagrams.

## Materials

- Bags of assorted buttons (one for each group)
- Yarn or string dividers
- Bags of small sea shells (one for each group)

## Student Actions

Students are faced with three problems.

### Problem 1

Sort your bag of buttons. Try to sort them at least 10 different ways. To ensure that students sort in as many ways as possible, teachers can *use a tiered approach.* The advanced button sorter is faced with this problem: If you were selling these buttons to a button collector, you would need to assign them different values.

- Assign each button group a value.
- Explain how much each button is worth.
- How did you decide on the values of the buttons? (Your thinking should also explain the specific facts about the buttons.)
- Weigh and measure the buttons.
- Play "Guess My Button" game (similar to "Twenty Questions").
- Understand the many meanings of the word buttons: elevator buttons, buttons on Web sites, car-lock buttons, alarm clock buttons, microwave buttons.
- Literature Connection: *Frog and Toad Are Friends* by Arnold Lobel (1970). Read the story "The Lost Button."

### Problem 2

Make a Venn Diagram using your bag of buttons. A Venn diagram is a method of illustrating set unions and intersections. For example, a set of blue buttons is one category, a set of round buttons is another category. A set of blue round buttons is an intersecting category.

A tiered challenge approach is used here. All students make a Venn diagram. For beginners, a Venn diagram can be divided into three sections. More advanced learners compare and contrast the different intersections. Question: "How did you decide which category a particular button fit into?"

Evaluate your selections. As a final activity, have students create a Venn diagram in a new and different way.

### Problem 3

Classify the shells by seriation. For example, sort from light to dark (color), from small to large, by the number of ridges, or by the amount of water each shell can hold.

For beginners, students seriate by color, size, and texture gradations.

This activity can also be tiered by challenge. Have advanced students become shell sorters, predicting ways the shells were used by the animals who once lived inside them. Students provide the reasons for the different shell shapes based on their reasoning. Students hypothesize and investigate their shells. In concluding, students evaluate and explain their shell organization process.

## Ways To Differentiate Instruction

The students work in groups to sort and classify the buttons ten different ways. The teachers differentiate learning materials, making sure students can classify, sort, and find as many ways as possible. He or she adapts instruction as students create a Venn diagram. The teachers want students to have as many chances as possible to find patterns, make comparisons, and figure out what intersection means. Teachers model examples, help students distinguish what is alike and different, and encourage group participation. In the final problem, students seriate shells and use a tiered approach

# Activity 2:
# Unknown Liquids Experiment (Grades 3–6)

## Inquiry Skills

Hypothesizing, experimenting, and communicating.

## Science Standards

Inquiry, physical science, science and technology, personal perspectives, written communications.

## Description

In this exploring activity, students are experimenting with chemicals and doing physical science work. They are learning to use tools found in the lab and becoming familiar with the safety rules of science, mathematics, and technology.

## Materials (for Each Table)

- 5 plastic containers
- 5 liquids (oil, water, soap, alcohol, vinegar)
- 5 medicine droppers
- 1 beaker
- 1 small plastic beaker
- 1 tray
- 1 sheet of plastic wrap
- 1 sheet of aluminum foil
- 1 sheet of waxed paper

**Procedures**

1. Set up the containers with liquids.
2. Discuss the colored liquids.
3. Set up the trays with papers and materials for each group (5 eye droppers, 2 beakers, 1 small plastic container)
4. On the board list some possible experiments with liquids:
   - Liquid races
   - Floatability
   - Density
   - Mixing liquids
   - Other ideas?

## Problem

Try to discover what the four liquids are.

Rules:

- ◆ Each liquid is a household substance that may or may not have been colored with food coloring to hide its identity.

- ◆ Students are limited to using only their sense of sight to do this experiment. Students should experiment by manipulating the liquids.

- ◆ For safety reasons, caution students they are not to smell, touch, or taste the chemicals.

- ◆ Each medicine dropper may be used to pick up only one liquid. We do not want contamination!

## Group Task

This lesson uses a *learning center model*. Students rotate among the centers. Student teams experiment trying to discover what the mystery liquids are. Flexible teams are formed where students work at their own pace. They perform a variety of tests as they rotate through the five centers.

## Group Actions

### *Center 1: Liquid Races*

- ◆ Choose a paper (aluminum foil, waxed paper, plain white paper, plastic wrap) and a liquid (red, green, blue, yellow, clear).

**Procedures**

1. Cover a tray with a paper of your choice.
2. With an eyedropper, put a drop of each liquid onto the paper.

3. Tip the tray to see which liquid moves the fastest.

4. Try the experiment with all the papers and all the liquids.

## Center 2: Floatability

♦ Use a small plastic container, add drops of each colored liquid.

♦ You want to see which liquid will float.

♦ Each student has a chance to experiment.

♦ Shake, tip, and maneuver the container to see which liquid moves to the top.

## Center 3: Density

♦ Use a small plastic container, add drops of each colored liquid.

♦ You want to see which liquid sinks.

♦ Each student has a chance to experiment.

♦ Shake, tip, and maneuver the container to see which liquid sinks.

## Center 4: Mixing Liquids

♦ Guess what each liquid is and test your guesses by observing which liquids mix together. Write your guesses:

blue liquid: _____        reasons: _____

green liquid: _____        reasons: _____

red liquid: _____        reasons: _____

yellow liquid: _____        reasons: _____

clear liquid: _____        reasons: _____

♦ Which will mix? Write your guesses.

oil: _____        reasons: _____

soap: _____        reasons: _____

water: _____        reasons: _____

vinegar: _____        reasons: _____

alcohol: _____        reasons: _____

## Center 5: Other Ideas Group Reflections

Reflect on the lesson.

## Group Actions

Use a collaborative team approach.

1. Form a group of four to six students.

2. Each group is to try liquid races in Center 1 and answer these questions:
   - Write a description of the activity.

*Gearing Up*

♦ What were your hypotheses?

*Gearing Down*

♦ Describe the activity.
   - Explain how your group went about solving the problem.

*Gearing Up*

♦ Why do you think the liquids behaved the way they did?

*Gearing Down*

♦ Record what happened in the race.
   - Write what the group learned from the activity.

*Gearing Up*

♦ What do you know from past experience about each liquid?

*Gearing Down*

♦ Our group learned that each liquid has _____.
   - How do you think the lesson could be improved?

*Gearing Up and Gearing Down*

♦ Describe how your group worked collaboratively.
   - What do you want to learn more about?

## Suggestions for Differentiating Instruction

The students work together to try and figure out what the unknown liquids are. The teachers encourage a collaborative approach. They offer suggestions on the different ways students can apply the knowledge of what they know about common chemicals.

# Activity 3:
# Demonstrating the Behavior of Molecules
# (Grades 3–6)

## Inquiry Skills

Observing, comparing, hypothesizing, experimenting, and communicating.

## Science Standards

Inquiry, physical science, science and technology, personal perspectives, written communications.

# Background Information Description

This activity simulates how molecules are connected to each other and the effect of temperature change on molecules. Students usually have questions about the way things work: "Why does ice cream melt?" "Why does the tea kettle burn my hand?" "Where does steam come from?" and "Why is it so difficult to break rocks?" Explain that molecules and atoms are the building blocks of matter. Heat and cold energy can change molecular form.

This is a hands-on demonstration of how molecules work as well as a great opportunity for students to participate and, perhaps, assume leadership as a group leader. Before beginning the demonstration, explain that matter and energy exist and can be changed, but not created or destroyed. Ask for volunteers to role play the parts of molecules.

## Student Actions

1. Join hands showing how molecules are connected to each other, explaining that these molecules represent matter in a solid form.

2. "Show what happens when a solid becomes a liquid."

   Heat causes the molecules to move more rapidly so that they can no longer hold themselves together. You should drop hands and started to wiggle and move around to show the liquid state.

3. "How do you think molecules act when they become a gas?"

   Carefully move students to the generalization that heat transforms solids into liquids and then into gases. The class enjoys watching the other students wiggle and fly around as they assume the role of molecules turning into a gas.

4. "What do you think will happen when the temperature drops to freezing?"

   The last part of the demonstration shows the idea than when an object is frozen, the molecules have stopped moving altogether. The demonstration and follow-up questions usually spark a lot of discussion and more questions.

# Suggested Ways to Differentiate Instruction

Interest and student motivation are paramount in this activity. Challenge students to discover how molecules are everywhere. The students are part of a hands-on demonstration trying to answer their questions about molecules. The teachers modify instruction when they ask for volunteers to play the role of molecules even though they want all students to participate. Collaborative group work is encouraged. Lots of discussion and communication take place in this differentiated hands-on activity.

In this activity, a collaborative model is used. The activity can be tiered by complexity gearing up for advanced learners.

*Gearing Up*

♦ Find examples of states of solid matter, liquids, and gases.

♦ Explain some real-life experiences, like rain in springtime or icicles in winter.

♦ Write an essay about the states of matter. It can be comical or serious.

*Gearing Down*

♦ The activity can be geared down by having students role-play becoming molecules.

# Activity 4:
# What Will Float? (Grades 3–6)

## Inquiry Skills

Hypothesizing, experimenting, and communicating.

## Science Standards

Inquiry, physical science, science and technology, personal perspectives, written communications.

## Description

The weight of water gives it pressure. The deeper the water, the more pressure there is. Pressure is also involved when something floats. For an object to float, opposing balanced forces work against each other. Gravity pulls down on the object, and the water pushes it up. The solution to floating is the object's size relevant to its weight. If it has a high volume and is light for its size, then, it has a large surface area for the water to push against. In this activity, students will explore what objects will float in water. All students should try to float some of these objects.

## Materials

- Large plastic bowl or aquarium
- Salt
- Bag of small objects to test (paper clip, nail, block, key, etc.)
- Ruler
- Spoon
- Oil-based modeling clay
- Paper towels
- Large washers
- Kitchen foil (6-inch square)

## Student Actions

1. Fill a plastic bowl half full with water.
2. Empty the bag of objects onto the table along with the other items.
3. Separate the objects into two groups: the objects that you think will float and the objects that will sink.
4. Record your predictions in your science/math journal.
5. Experiment by trying to float all the floating objects.
6. Try the ones you think will sink.
7. Record what happened in your science/math journal.

## *Evaluation*

- When groups finish the activities, have them analyze and evaluate.
- In this tiered activity, students are working with physics. Topics such as pressure, volume, weight, gravity, rafts, boats, and swimming safety should all be discussed.

## Group Actions

### *Gearing Up*

- Explain your answers by giving examples of things you've experienced. For example, scuba divers face issues like these.
- Explain in descriptive terms.
- Write a fictional story or real-life experience about floating and sinking.

### *Gearing Down*

Think about these questions and come up with a group response:

- What is alike about all the objects that floated? Sank?
- What can be done to sink the objects that floated?
- What can be done to float the objects that sank?
- In what ways can a piece of foil be made to float? Sink?
- Describe how a foil boat can be made.
- How many washers do you think the foil boat will carry?
- What do you think could float in salt water that cannot float in freshwater?
- Try to find something that will float in fresh water and sink in saltwater. Take a guess.

## Differentiated Instruction Suggestions

For this lesson, a workshop model is used where open ended tasks are adjusted as the teacher interacts with small groups. Teachers introduce the purpose of the activity. Students have fun experimenting with what will float. Students construct boats made from aluminum foil. This motivating activity looks at water pressure, gravity, volume, weight, and ways to solve problems. Teachers differentiate by making it clear what students are to learn; understand, appreciate, and build on student differences; and adjust content, process, and product in response to student readiness, interests, and learning profile.

# Activity 5:
# Water Cohesion and Surface Tension
# (Grades 2–5)

## Inquiry Skills

Hypothesizing, experimenting, and communicating.

## Science Standards

Inquiry, earth science, science and technology, personal perspectives, written communications.

## Description

Students determine how many drops of water will fit on a penny in an experiment that demonstrates water cohesion and surface tension.

## Materials

- One penny for each pair of students
- Glasses of water
- Paper towels
- Eye droppers (one for each pair of students)

## Student Actions

1. Work with a partner.
2. Guess how many drops of water will fit on the penny.
3. Record your guesses on the chalkboard.
4. Turn the penny over and guess again.
5. Record what happened.

## Teacher Actions

Introduce the concept of cohesion. (Cohesion is the attraction of like molecules for each other. In solids and liquids, the force is strongest. It is cohesion that holds a solid or liquid together. There is also an attraction among water molecules for each other.) Introduce and discuss the idea of surface tension. (The molecules of water on the surface hold together so well that they often keep heavier objects from breaking through. The surface acts as if it is covered with skin.)

## Evaluation, Completion, and /or Follow-up

Have students explain how this activity showed surface tension. Instruct students to draw what surface tension looked like in their science/math journal. What makes the water drop break on the surface of the penny? (It is gravity.) What other examples can students think of where water cohesion can be observed? (Rain on a car windshield or window in a classroom, for example.) Even disinterested students can relate to this activity if drawn into the conversation.

## Differentiated Instruction Suggestions

The teachers differentiate by modifying instruction based on their ongoing assessment of students' science knowledge. They explain what students are to learn and give them opportunities to work with a partner. Students observe, ask questions, discuss, and record their findings. Writing about surface tension is an important follow-up activity.

This collaborative activity uses a collaborative model. Water cohesion and surface tension is tiered by complexity.

### Gearing Up

♦ Have students formulate assumptions; examine and support their ideas; and hypothesize, represent, or demonstrate ideas in a new way rather than simply listing or applying another's ideas.

### Gearing Down

♦ Record your questions and write your responses.

# Activity 6: Experimenting With Surface Tension (Grades 3–8)

## Inquiry Skills

Hypothesizing, experimenting, and communicating.

## Science Standards

Inquiry, physical science, science and technology, personal perspectives, written communications.

## Description

Students develop an understanding that technological solutions to problems, such as phosphate-containing detergents, have intended benefits and may have unintended consequences.

## Objective

Students apply their knowledge of surface tension. This experiment shows how water acts like it has a stretchy skin because water molecules are strongly attracted to each other. Students can also watch how soap molecules squeeze between the water molecules, pushing them apart, and reducing the water's surface tension

## How Do You Differentiate?

Stations are different spaces in the classroom where students work on various tasks simultaneously. The stations in this activity are divided by the materials being used. Station one uses whole milk, station two uses skim milk, station three uses 1% milk, station four uses half-and-half, and station five uses water.

Students follow procedures 1 through 3 and record their findings. Discussions with the class usually involve the discussions of variables and how the results changed from station to station. Not all students need to spend the same amount of time in each station. Even when all students go to every station, assignments may vary.

## Background Information

Milk, which is mostly water, has surface tension. When the surface of milk is touched with a drop of soap, the surface tension of the milk is reduced at that spot. Because the surface tension of the milk at the soapy spot is much weaker than it is in the rest of the milk, the water molecules elsewhere in the bowl pull water molecules away from the soapy spot. The movement of the food coloring reveals these currents in the milk.

## Grouping

Divide class into groups of four or five students.

## Materials

- Milk (only whole or 2% will work)
- Newspapers
- Shallow container
- Food coloring
- Dishwashing soap
- Saucer or plastic lid
- Toothpicks

### Procedures

1. Take the milk out of the refrigerator half an hour before the experiment starts.
2. Place the dish on the newspaper and pour about half an inch of milk into the dish.

3. Let the milk sit for a minute or two.

## Student Actions

1. Near the side of the dish, put 1 drop of food coloring in the milk. Place a few colored drops in a pattern around the dish. What happened?
2. Pour some dishwashing soap into the plastic lid. Dip the end of the toothpick into the soap, and touch it to the center of the milk. What happened?
3. Dip the toothpick into the soap again, and touch it to a blob of color. What happened?
4. Rub soap over the bottom half of a food coloring bottle. Stand the bottle in the middle of the dish. What happened?

The colors can move for about 20 minutes when students keep dipping the toothpick into the soap and touching the colored drops.

## Follow-up Evaluation

Students discuss their findings and share their outcomes with other groups. Using stations adds another dimension. Have students record their findings and explain why their results turned out as they did.

## Suggested Alternatives for Differentiated Instruction

When delivering instruction, there are many avenues to creating an instructionally responsive classroom. As you read about instructional strategies in this chapter, observe how teachers can use them to create classrooms where students have the opportunity to work at a comfortable pace, at an individually challenging degree of difficulty, and at a learning mode that is a good match for their learning profiles.

Stations are different spaces in the class where students work on various tasks simultaneously. The stations in this activity can be divided by the materials being used. Station one uses whole milk, station two uses skim milk, station three uses half-and-half, and station four uses water. Students follow the procedures 1 through 8 and record their findings. Discussions with class members usually involve the discussion of variables (in this case materials being used, such as milk) and how the results changed from station to station. Not all students need to spend the same amount of time in each station. Even when all students go to every station, assignments at each station may vary.

# Activity 7:
# Create a Static Electric Horse
# (Grades 3–6)

## Inquiry Skills

Hypothesizing, experimenting, and communicating.

## Science Standards

Inquiry, physical science, science and technology, personal perspectives, written communications.

## Objectives and Description

- ◆ Students have an opportunity to explore static electricity.
- ◆ No previous knowledge of static electricity is necessary.
- ◆ Students learn through fun and hands-on experimentation about the concepts of static electricity (i.e., positive and negative charges).

## Materials

- 1 inflated balloon for each student
- Scissors
- Tag board horse patterns
- Colored tissue paper
- Crayons and/or markers

### Procedures

1. Short introduction focusing on the horses and a mystery question: Ask students if they think they could make a paper horse move without touching it? (No mention yet of static electricity concepts.)
2. Teachers describe how to construct the horse.

## Student Actions

1. Fold the paper in half and trace the horse pattern on one side of tissue paper. (Trace forms are passed out by the teacher.)
2. Fold both halves of tissue paper together and cut out the pattern, making sure to leave the horse joined together at the top of its head and tail.
3. Decorate (color) both sides of the horse.
4. The teacher describes how to *electrify* the paper horse.
5. Place your horse on a smooth surface.
6. Rub a balloon over your hair a few times.
7. Hold the balloon in front of the horse.

8. The teachers pass out the balloons.

9. Next, the teachers instruct the students to get in groups of four or five sitting around the table.

10. Now, students *electrify* their horses and have short races across the tables.

11. After the races have ended, have a class discussion on what happened between balloon and horse.

12. Ask students to describe their views. Then, add the scientific explanation describing static electricity:

    - The outer layer of electrons from atoms on the hair are rubbed off and cling to the atoms of the balloon, producing static electricity. When students hold the positively charged balloon close to the uncharged (negatively charged) horse, there is a strong attraction between them. The horse races toward the balloon.

## Evaluation

Write up an evaluation of the activity.

### Student Actions

1. Write in your journal about the experiment.

2. *For advanced learners*: Explain the connection between the horse, balloon, and static electricity.

    - Write an article for the school newspaper describing the experiment
    - Illustrate the *electric* horse race, provide commentary.

3. *For students finding it hard* to write about "their horse" or afraid to construct a horse for themselves.

    - Work with a small group and come up with a group statement of the experiment.
    - Write a short story about your horse in the race.

## Assessment

Assessment is based on observing the students and reading their written/illustrated journals about their experiments.

# Activity 8:
# Rain Forest Interdependence (Grades K–2)

## Inquiry Skills

Hypothesizing, experimenting, and communicating.

## Science Standards

Inquiry, life science, science and technology, personal perspectives, written communications.

## Description

This inclusive science activity is designed for all students, but it's an ideal lesson to use for limited English proficient (LEP) learners. It encourages the students to come together and establish themselves as groups; speaking and writing are not mandatory! The only adaptation required in this activity is a simple color coding of the identifying cards, which enables the student to visualize what other students (plants and animals) he or she is connected with, rather than just reading the card. Additional adaptations might include pictures of the plant or animal on the cards that show the actual relationship, or more color coding, by matching the color of the yarn to the color of the cards. The student can see group members by the colors, pictures, and yarns, and understand the interrelationships, without having to read the card.

This is a valuable lesson for LEP students as well as students with other language deficiencies and all students within the classroom. The exceptional student not be singled out, and all the students can benefit by the simple color classification. The color coding and pictures serve to reinforce the written relationships, and the students receive graphic, physical examples of the purpose of the activity to show interdependence. The activity helps increase social interaction within the classroom and might help break down the barrier caused by the difference in language.

The evaluation and conclusion to this activity is for students to discuss and then write their reaction to, or interpretation of, what occurred when the connections were broken. This is an opportunity for the student and their classmates to artistically describe the lesson.

## Objectives

♦ Students follow directions, participate in all activities, and work cooperatively with their classmates.

♦ Students discuss, as a class their feelings about this activity.

♦ Students draw a picture of the interdependence of the rain forest.

♦ Students use some of the information that has been gained in the previous lessons.

## Materials

- Plant and animal cards pasted on 3 × 5 index cards
- Pictures of rain forest plants and animals
- Yarn (3-yard pieces) for 3 pieces per student
- Paper and other art supplies

## Preparation

♦ Teachers, aides, or student helpers cut and paste pictures of plant and animal cards onto 3 × 5 cards for each student.

♦ Pictures or books of rain forest plants and animals should be available for reference if needed.

♦ Move the desks to the edges of the classroom, so that the students can move around.

## Student Actions

1. Get a card and pieces of yarn from your teacher.
2. Read your card and then, find the other people that match your card.
3. When a match is made, attach yourselves together with a long piece of yarn (tied around your wrist).
4. Remember, more than two can be connected. Example: Kapok tree will be attached to parrots, insects, and so forth.

# Evaluation

♦ *For advanced learners*: Discuss how it feels to depend on the others.

♦ *For students having trouble*: Guess what part of the rain forest your plant or animal lives in: canopy, under story, or forest floor.

♦ *All students reflect on these questions*:

- What plant or animal did you represent?
- What do you depend on for food or shelter?
- How does it feel to have so many connections?
- What did you learn from this activity?
- Would you like to live in a rain forest? Why
- What would happen if the Kapok tree is cut down?
- What other animals would be affected?

## Suggested Ways to Differentiate Instruction

The teachers can differentiate instruction by modifying instruction based on their knowledge of the topic. They implement the children's book *The Great Kopok Tree: A Tale of the Amazon Rain Forest* by Lynne Cherry (1990). This a story of a young man chopping down a great Kapok tree in the rain forest. He becomes tired and falls asleep. One by one, the animals who live around the tree emerge to beg him not to destroy their home. As the teacher continues to read, students pay close attention to the animals hidden in the foliage. Ask children to predict what will happen next. There are a host of exciting possibilities for teaching young readers. Things to do after reading, art, drama, science, conservation, and environmental issues all come into play.

## Possible Direct Instruction Suggestions

Teachers can use tiered activities, so all students focus on basic understandings and skills but at different levels of complexity. By keeping the focus of the activity the same, but offering ways of access at varying degrees of difficulty, the teacher gets the most out of each student; each student comes away with essential skills and each student is appropriately challenged. Another way to differentiate is to modify students' products (in this case, constructions). Teachers should provide for students who need concrete structures *and* those who do well with structures that are quite complex.

# Summary and Conclusion

Differentiated science instruction pays close attention to who we teach, the content, and how we teach it. It is a model that acknowledges the importance of standards, but also demonstrates how meaning and understanding can originate from the structure of the content standards so that students develop powers of mind as well as build up an information base. At its best, science instruction nurtures the creative spirit in all students as they develop and deepen their understanding of the subject. By encouraging the exploration of each student's interests, strengths, and learning preferences, everyone's work is honored.

How students come to understand and take ownership of knowledge is shown when students apply what they have learned in everyday situations. In the differentiated classroom, science is often made more meaningful by relating what is being learned to real life situations. Effective teachers provide plenty of opportunities for students to explore, identify, interpret, and apply knowledge. Efforts are valued and students are often encouraged to assess themselves. Active science learning connects students with the natural world of the past, present, and future. Unleashing the power of knowledgeable teachers means building up their informal ideas and judgments to invent the science classrooms of the future.

Now, more than ever, the science curriculum pays close attention to responsible citizenship and self-understanding. To some degree, the science curriculum can reflect human values and emphasize responsibility by helping students realize that they are part of a global community. Related curriculum goals include using scientific knowledge in making wise decisions and solving difficult problems related to life and living. In a whole host of ways, science is becoming more interdisciplinary; for example, some emerging research fields include biochemistry, biophysics, plant engineering, terrestrial biology, and neurobiology, to name a few. Although understanding the natural world is still the focus, science now recognizes dimensions that extend from digital technology to the social sciences—as well as ethics, values, and law.

From our experience, it helps to meet the needs of all of the students in a classroom if you can find interesting relationships between science and students' life experiences. Learning how to learn also helps prepare students for the world in which they will live. Educators recognize that the time has come to develop curricula in a way that no longer isolates science from human welfare and social and economic progress. Meeting the adaptive needs of students in a changing world is part of what today's science education is about. But no matter how you vary instruction, the central focus for teachers is replacing naive conceptions and lack of knowledge about science by helping students construct more accurate and complete understandings. To differentiate science lessons and experiences, teachers formally and informally assess their students' capabilities with respect to multiple intelligences and preferred learning styles.

# References and Resources

Adams, D., & Hamm, M. (2005). *Redefining education in the twenty-first century: Shaping collaborative learning in the age of information.* Springfield, IL: Charles C. Thomas Publisher.

American Association for the Advancement of Science. (2001). *Atlas of science literacy.* Washington, DC: Author.

Benjamin, A. (2003). *Differentiated Instruction: A guide for elementary school teachers.* Larchmont, NY: Eye On Education.

Benjamin, A. (2002). *Differentiated instruction: A guide for middle and high school teachers.* Larchmont, NY: Eye On Education.

Bloom, B. (Ed.). (1984). *Taxonomy of educational objectives: Book 1—Cognitive domain.* Reading, MA: Addison Wesley.

Brandt, R. (Ed.) (2000). Education in a new era. In *Association for Supervision and Curriculum Development Yearbook 2000.* Alexandria, VA: ASCD.

Center for the Study of Teaching and Policy. (2001). *Teacher preparation research: Current knowledge, gaps, and recommendations.* Seattle, WA: Author.

Gaga, P. (1994). *Science in elementary education* (7th ed.). New York: Macmillan.

Glatthorn, A., & Jailall, J. (2000). Curriculum for the new millennium. In Brandt. R. (Ed.), *Education in a new era: ASCD Year book 2000.* Alexandria, VA: ASCD.

Gilbert, J., and Kotelman, M. (2005). Five good reasons to use science notebooks. *Science & Children, 43*(3), 28–32.

Greene, B. (2003). *The elegant universe.* New York: Vintage Books.

Hamm, M., & Adams, D. (1998). *Literacy in science, technology and the language arts: An interdisciplinary inquiry.* Westport, CN: Bergin & Garvey.

Howe, A. (2000). *Engaging children in science.* Upper Saddle River, NJ: Merrill-Prentice-Hall.

Jackson, A. W., & Davis, G. A. (2000). *Turning points 2000: Educating adolescents in the 21st century.* New York: Teachers College Press.

Multiple Intelligence Links Pages: ss.uno.edu/SS/Theory/MultintelLks.html/.

National Academy Press (1996). *National science education standards.* Washington, DC: National Academy Press.

National Research Council (NRC). (2000). *Inquiry and the national science education standards.* Washington, DC: National Academy Press.

Online Learning Styles Inventory: www.metamath.com/Isweb/dvclearn.htm/.

Paulos, J. A. (1991). *Beyond Numeracy.* New York: Alfred Knopf.

Pine, J., & Aschbacher, P. (2006). Students' learning of inquiry in "inquiry" curricula. *Phi Delta Kappa, 88*(4), 308–313.

Schultz, J. (January 2002). Learning how to learn: Science education for struggling students. *Quest, 5*(1), 1–3.

Sherman, H., Richardson, L., & Yard, G. (2005). *Teaching children who struggle with mathematics: A systematic approach to analysis and correction.* Upper Saddle River: NJ: Pearson Prentice Hall.

Science Myths: www.amasci.com/miscon/miscon.html/.

Thomas, E. (2003). *Styles and strategies for teaching middle school mathematics* (2nd ed.) Ho-Ho-Kus, NJ: Thoughtful Education Press.

Tomlinson, C. (1999) *The differentiated classroom: Responding to the needs of all learners.* Alexandria, VA: Association for Supervision and Curriculum Development.

Tomlinson, C., Cunningham Eidson, C. (2003). *Differentiation in practice: A resource guide for differentiating curriculum.* Alexandria, VA: Association for Supervision and Curriculum Development.

Weiss, I., & Pasley, J. (February 2004). What is quality instruction? *Educational Leadership, 61*(5), 24–28.

- For a more challenging questions: "How many Skittles will fit in a square mile?"
- "How many Skittles will fit in a 48,000 square football field?"

### *Gearing Down*

- We know there are 144 Skittles in a 6-inch square; how many are there in a square foot? (A square foot is 12 inches on all four sides and 24 Skittles can be placed along each side, so the area is $24 \times 24 = 576$.)

## Assessment

Have students pass in their worksheets and check for understanding.

# Geometry

## Lesson Plan 9: Angles Merry-Go-Round

*With Nicole Brown and Neema Oserga-McCockran*

**Topic:** Geometry (measuring angles)

**Grade level:** 4

**Objectives**

- ♦ *What you want students to learn*: Students find angles in the real world; compare and name angles.

- ♦ *Why are the concepts important?* Students begin to learn the basic ideas of geometry and realize that angles are all around us.

- ♦ *What background information do students need before starting?* Students should discuss and recognize angles all around them (the corner of your book is one example; many examples of angles should be discussed, however).

- ♦ *Organization and Procedures*: This activity takes several class sessions. Student partners make a merry-go-round using an overhead transparency formed in a circle over paper covered cardboard. The transparency has a marked vortex in the center and points A, B, C, and D marked on the outer edges of the circle. One push pin is placed on the vortex. Pairs of students take turns spinning the merry-go-round. When it stops after the first student's spin, have the student place a push pin in the spot and label it point D. This leaves a mark on the paper. Repeat the step. Now, each pair has two points. Once lines are drawn, an angle is created.

**Materials**

- Paper, cardboard
- Push pins
- Ruler
- Compass
- Transparency
- Pencil and fine markers

**How Are You Going to Get the Students Involved?**

Students work as a partnership to play the mathematical merry-go-round game.

**Lesson Development, Questions, and Results**

Students discuss the different sizes of angles and how they can be produced.

**Small Group Options**

Students form a group of two.

### Gearing Up

- Have students use a compass to measure the angles.
- Label each angle.
- Find angles in the classroom (your desk, the door, the chalk board, and so on). Record each angle.
- Predict how many spins it will take to form a 90-degree angle, a 60-degree angle, a 120-degree angle, and so on.

### Gearing Down

- Have students spin and draw different angles.
- List all the angles that are corner angles.
- Tell a story about a merry-go-round.
- Did you ever ride on a merry-go-round? Describe your experience.

## Assessment (Observations, Products Produced, Portfolio Entry)

Observation is a good assessment strategy for this lesson. Have students write and compare different angles in their portfolio.

# Life Science

## Lesson Plan 10: Tooth Health

*With Alexandra Ott and Bet "Ellen" Heyward*

**Topic:** Dental hygiene

**Grade level:** K–5

**Objectives**

+ *What you want students to learn*: Students learn the importance of properly brushing and flossing their teeth and the effects of bacteria on teeth.

+ *Why are the concepts important?* Students learn about proper techniques for healthier hygiene results. Students become familiar with the anatomy of the mouth.

+ *What background information do students need before starting?* Students must recognize that cleanliness prevents infections and illness.

---

### Organization and Procedures

♦ Students are shown slides of bad and good teeth.

♦ Teachers explain basic science behind plaque and gum disease.

♦ Teacher demonstrates good cleaning habits.

♦ Students practice brushing and flossing.

**Materials**

• Disposable toothbrushes (can get from dental office, usually provided free)

• Pocket mirrors to look at teeth

• Model sculpture of teeth (for teacher)

### How Are You Going to Get the Students Involved?

This is a hands-on activity. Students are actively involved in finding out about tooth hygiene and applying directions for teeth and gum cleaning.

### Lesson Development, Questions, and Desired Product

Explain teeth health step by step:

♦ Eating: chemicals break down food.

♦ Saliva is part of the process.

♦ Plaque are particles between teeth which can lead to cavities.

♦ Bacteria are microscopic but often can form from cavities.

♦ Explain steps in proper brushing and flossing to avoid plaque and cavities.

## Small Group Options

Students can practice with each other using toothbrushes and pocket mirrors.

### Gearing Up

- Extension of student vocabulary (dental hygiene, bacteria).
- Create a chart showing the steps of tooth decay.
- Write a letter explaining how to take care of your teeth.
- Use creative drama showing what happens when cavities form.
- Practice flossing and brushing, explain the steps you used.
- Suggest healthy eating habits that are tooth friendly.
- Design a handout showing the directions for teeth and gum cleaning.

### Gearing Down

- Have pairs of students practice brushing and flossing.
- Use pocket mirrors to observe your teeth.
- Keep a record of when you brush and floss your teeth.

## Assessment (Observations, Products Produced, Portfolio Entry)

- Teacher observation is a good assessment strategy for this lesson.
- Have students write about teeth health in their portfolio.

## Lesson Plan 11: Fruity Fall Delights

*With Nessa Hessami and Lyne Cvadra*

**Topic:** Three fall fruits

**Grade level:** K–2

**Objectives**

- *What you want students to learn*: Students classify different fruits (same and different) and compare and contrast each fruit.
- *Why are the concepts important?* It helps students sort facts and organize information.
- *What background information do students need before starting?* Students must have eaten, seen, or touched pumpkins, apples, and oranges.

---

### Organization and Procedures

Give each group a pumpkin, an apple, and an orange. Ask them to describe each fruit. How are they alike? How are they different?

**Materials**

- Poster paper
- Markers and crayons
- Thinking cap

**How Are You Going to Get the Students Involved?**

- Bring in the three fruits: apples, oranges, and pumpkins.
- Encourage students to compare the fruits by drawing a picture about them.
- Ask students to look at things that are similar about the fruits.
- Next, have students list the differences.
- Students can, then, make a chart of what they found.

**Lesson Development, Questions, and Desired Product**

To understand how apples, oranges, and pumpkins are different but similar.

**Small Group Options**

Two people in a group working together.

*Gearing Up*

- Encourage students to compare the apples, oranges, and pumpkins with other fruits such as bananas, pears, and grapes.
- Write how they were alike and how they were different.
- Add a strawberry or oddly shaped fruit such as a pineapple.

- Divide into centers. The orange center, apple center, and pumpkin center.
  - The orange center divides the peeled orange.
  - The apple center is in charge of getting an apple ready for baking.
  - The pumpkin center is helped to get the seeds out of the pumpkin.
- Next, students help prepare three fruit treats (e.g., dividing an orange, cleaning pumpkin seeds for roasting, preparing apples for baking, etc.).

### Gearing Down

Use only two fruits to compare.

- Each student participates in a center (a teacher assistant helps students out).
- Help peel oranges and bananas.
- Help clean out the inside of the pumpkin and separate the seeds.
- Get the apples ready for baking (sugar, cinnamon, water, and whole cored apples).

### Assessment (Observations, Products Produced, Portfolio Entry)

- Students can make a fun diagram based on the fall fruits.
- Areas such as nutrition, math, and science concepts fit in easily.
- Students can also look at fall vegetables and make comparisons.
- Students help prepare the fall fruit snacks:
  - The pumpkin seeds are salted and baked.
  - The orange is dished up.
  - The apples are baked for the class and dished up.
- Teacher *observation* is a good way to assess this activity.
- Have students write and classify the fruits in their portfolio.

## Recipes for Fruity Fall Delights

### Baked Apples

Wash 4 large tart apples. Remove cores to 1/2 inch of bottoms, then cut a strip of peel from the hollowed ends. Mix 1/4 cup of sugar, 1 teaspoon of cinnamon. Set in pan with 3/4 cup of hot water. Cover and bake for 45 to 60 minutes until tender. Serve hot or cold.

### Pumpkin Seeds

Bake 2 cups of pumpkin seeds in 2 teaspoons of butter at 300 degrees Fahrenheit for 15 minutes. Watch carefully so they do not burn. While hot from the oven, sprinkle with salt.

### Orange Fruit Salad

2 oranges, 2 apples, 2 bananas

Cut up fruit and mix together in large bowl. The juice from the oranges help keep the apples from turning brown. Prepare just before serving.

# Earth Science

Earth science resources are rocks and soils, water, and gases of the atmosphere. The sun, moon, stars, clouds, birds and airplanes all have properties that can be observed and described.

## Lesson Plan 12: Gases Everywhere

*Adapted from American Chemical Society, 2001; with Andrea Eng*

**Topic:** Gas pressure

**Grade level:** 3–5

**Materials**

- Gallon-sized zip closing plastic freezer bags
- Plastic flexible straws
- Books
- Beach ball

**Objectives**

Students know what gas pressure is. Students understand the relationship between gas and pressure (adding gas increases pressure, removing gas decreases pressure).

**Introduction**

1. Hold up a beach ball and have a few volunteers come squeeze the ball. Ask them if it was easy or hard to squeeze?

2. Now, let a little air out and have them squeeze the ball again. Easy or hard to squeeze?

3. Explain what pressure is (a force exerted by a substance on another substance).

4. Explain what gas pressure is (the pressure of a gas is the force that the gas exerts on the walls of its container). As the pressure increases, the gas pushes harder and harder against the inside of the container.

---

### Model/Procedures

Pass out plastic bags and straws. Have students follow along as the teacher demonstrates the activity.

1. Place the plastic bag near the edge of the table. Close the bag except for a small spot in the corner.

2. Put a straw into the bag with part of the flexible straw sticking out. Use your fingers to press down on both sides of the straw to keep the air from leaking out of the bag. Blow into the bag.

3. When the bag looks like a little pillow, take the straw out and seal the bag. What do you feel? Push down on the bag, the air pressure is pushing up on your hand.

4. *Put this pressure to work.* Let the air out of the bag and put the straw into the bag. Place a book on top of the bag.

### Gearing Down

♦ Blow into the bag. What happens to the book?

♦ Try lifting two books. How many books do you think you can lift with the power of pressure? Try it and see! Record what happened in your science journal.

### Gearing Up

Some real life examples include air bags found in most cars. The activity shows students how an air bag works.

♦ Can you think of other real life examples of air pressure?

♦ Explain why an air bag offers better protection for the driver or an air tank assists scuba divers.

### Assessment

Create an observation chart on gas pressure. Record guesses of how many books you can lift and actual amounts. Put your work in your portfolio.

# Lesson Plan 13: What We Do Adds Up!

*With Beth Jackson*

**Topic:** Environmental awareness math and science activities are offered that may help students better understand how their presence and actions can and do affect our world. Did you know that on average each person throws away about 4.4 pounds of trash every day?

**Grade level:** 4–6

## Objectives

Students become familiar with the environmental affect of throwing out trash. Students calculate the effects of adding garbage to their local environment.

## Word Problem Quick Quiz

- On average, how much does each person throw away in a week?

  Answer: 30.8 pounds

- On average, how long does it take for each person to throw away 100 pounds of garbage?

  Answer: 22.7 days

- On average, how much garbage will a person throw away this year?

  Answer: 1,601.6 pounds

- At this rate, would a person your age have contributed a ton of garbage? On average, how long does it take for each person to throw away a ton (2,000 pounds) of garbage?

  Answer: 22.7 days

- So far in your lifetime, about how much garbage have you contributed?

### Gearing Down

Landfills in the United States have charged between $10 and $100 per ton to dump trash. If it costs $20 per ton, estimate how much money will be spent this year.

### Gearing Up

Estimate what it would take to reduce the garbage in this class, in this city, in this country. Write a letter to the school newspaper voicing your views.

## Assessment

Students' understandings are based on their quiz answers.

# Physical Science

## Lesson Plan 14: Yo-Yo Physics

*With Kris Berry and Aiko Hatakeyama*

**Topic:** Gravity and yo-yos

**Grade level:** K–junior high

**Objectives**

- *What you want students to learn:* Students observe concepts about force, acceleration, friction, and gravity.

- *Why are the concepts important?* Students can apply physics to real world situations.

- *What background information do students need before starting?* Students should examine the principles of gravity and review basic physics concepts of inertia.

---

### Organization and Procedures

This activity takes one or two class periods. Pairs of students experiment with yo-yos. Students try to maneuver yo-yos in different ways.

**Materials**

- Yo-yos
- Math and science journal
- Pens

**How Are You Going to Get the Students Involved?**

Students work in pairs to play with their yo-yos. Hands-on involvement starts after instruction about how yo-yos work. The lesson challenges students to try to show how gravity works.

**Lesson Development, Questions, and Desired Product**

Allow students time to play with yo-yos, working in pairs. Discuss what they did during their free play time; how they maneuvered their yo-yos and what tricks they tried. Share different physics concepts that influence motion, speed, and direction.

**Small Group Options**

Groups of two work well with this activity.

*Gearing Up*

Have students estimate the different directions that the yo-yo moved during a period of time:

- ◆ Record the velocity (or rate of change of its position). Guess the speed at which the yo-yo traveled.
- ◆ What other objects that you know travel at a similar rate of speed?
- ◆ If you were to travel in a car from your house to school how many turns would you make?
- ◆ Draw a map of your car trip recording all turns.
- ◆ Can you think of an imaginary space vehicle that could travel at a similar rate of speed as the yo-yo. Write a short story about it.
- ◆ Write a short paragraph of how yo-yos show how gravity works?
- ◆ Give some examples of gravity.
- ◆ Why does a yo-yo behave as it does?
- ◆ There are some professional yo-yo groups. Go online to discover more about them. Record your findings.

### Gearing Down

Have students slow down the yo-yo and then, try to speed it up. Record the movements in your journal.

- ◆ Count the number of times your yo-yo went up and down.
- ◆ Describe the yo-yo motions you see.
- ◆ What causes the yo-yo to move?
- ◆ What directions does the yo-yo move when it is dropped?
- ◆ What happens when the yo-yo is thrown in a different direction?
- ◆ When does your yo-yo travel the fastest?
- ◆ What makes the yo-yo slow down?
- ◆ What might make the yo-yo move slower?
- ◆ Record the number of times your yo-yo went up and down when you slowed your yo-yo down.
- ◆ What happened when you made your yo-yo go faster?
- ◆ Compare with your partner.
- ◆ Make a group chart showing the slow and fast movements of your yo-yos.

### Assessment (Observations, Products Produced, Portfolio Entry)

- ◆ Have students write and describe the physics involved with yo-yos in their portfolio.
- ◆ With partners, ask students to describe the changing motions of a yo-yo using the vocabulary words: force, speed, gravity, and friction. Allow partners to help each other clarify explanations as they practice. Record on a class chart which students are able to successfully use the vocabulary in their explanation.

Promoter Executor™ · Being an ESTP

Temperament: **Improviser**™ · Interaction Style: **In-Charge**™ · Cognitive Processes: **Se, Ti, Fe, Ni | Si, Te, Fi, Ne**

## Dealing with Your Stress

As an outstanding, highly successful negotiator, trouble-shooter, and promoter, you will easily and quite effortlessly push all limits to achieve the desired results. However, when obstacles cannot be overcome, challenges are not adequately met, risks have not paid off, and objectives not achieved, the resulting experience can be like hitting a brick wall. This not only damages your overall confidence level, which gives rise to much anxiety, but can also lead to a feeling of being discredited and disrespected on a system-wide basis. You are naturally born with an unshakable confidence, coupled with an "in charge, set the goal, and go after it" attitude. As a result, when your confidence does get shaken or even damaged, it can leave you not only profoundly discouraged, but in a temporary state of confusion. Like a broken compass, you may react in context without a clear sense of direction. This can take on the look of doing more of the same, overdoing— creating a whirlwind of energy, denying the realities at hand, and/or creating distractions.

### Prescriptions for Stress

☞ Constantly review and reset desired goals and objectives in all areas.

☞ Find exercise programs that offer variety, simplicity, and pleasure. Those that involve groups of one or more other people are a particularly good option.

☞ With assistance and guidance, establish a healthy nutritional program, with moderation being the key to achieving success.

☞ Rechannel some social energies and talents into civic and/or professional arenas.

## How You Learn

You learn best when you have the freedom to tactically prioritize what to learn and when to learn it. You like taking charge of a situation and that includes your learning. Sometimes you'll even end up acting as a consultant to help the teacher, if you're given half a chance to respectfully show what you know. You remember an incredible amount of information if you know you'll have an opportunity to use it and see how it fits into what you have to do. You want to have a measure of how well you've performed.

## For Your Career Mastery

You'll move quickly to take advantage of currently available career options that offer lively challenges and some excitement. You will actively network with others and draw on past connections. You may miss opportunities that come from turning inward to explore long-term implications of career actions. Your energy, practicality, fun-loving nature, and flexibility are pluses. When connecting with others, you will sell yourself well, but be sure to communicate your serious and committed side, and be sure to let others talk during interviews. Resist the urge to take stopgap jobs that promise a quick change. You are excellent at gathering information through talking to others who have experience. You will logically and realistically weigh the pros and cons of career/job options but may neglect to evaluate the long-term potential of any given choice and may forget to weigh in your own most important life values. You have short-term tangible goals but may not have a long-term plan. You may have difficulty following through on plans that are made.

### Challenge Yourself

Clarify what is truly important to you in a career, develop a plan that takes into account your long-term career needs and the long-term potential of a job, and follow through on decisions and commitments.

## Reminders for Personal Growth

Noticing relevant evidence to quickly arrive at a reasoned action is your strength. Find ways to move ahead while maintaining the company of those close to you. Remember that others cannot go as fast as you or have as much confidence to just jump into things. Not everything should be measured or argued. When trying to convince or recruit others, you will get the most buy-in when your approach matches their values. Keep in mind that your talent for negotiating around or through problems can be misread as manipulation. Also, clients do not count as friends, people respond well to curiosity, and disagreement is not disrespect. In relationships, give others generous opportunities to exercise being in charge too. Remember how much impact you can make problem solving with a team. When you win people over, they want follow through. Exploring the subtleties of life's philosophical questions is its own reward. Respect is best earned through wisdom. You don't need to be conventional—your creativity will win in the end.

Temperament: **Improviser**™ · Interaction Style: **Chart-the-Course**™ · Cognitive Processes: **Ti, Se, Ni, Fe | Te, Si, Ne, Fi**

## Snapshot

Theme is action-driven problem solving. Their talents lie in using frameworks for solving problems. They often excel at operating all kinds of tools and instruments. Keen observers of the environment, they are a storehouse of data and facts relevant to analyzing and solving problems. They thrive on challenging situations and having the freedom to craft clever solutions and do whatever it takes to fix things and make them work. They take pride in their skill and virtuosity, which they seem to effortlessly acquire.

## When Solving Problems

They decide quickly when responding to immediate need, but slowly when they don't see options for action. They're constantly observing, taking in a lot of concrete information, and looking for all the angles. They like to see if the facts fit together, try something, and see what happens. They respond to the needs of the moment when new information comes in that will make something work more efficiently but prefer to enter a situation having analyzed it first. To influence them, give them the rationale for the change that is needed and move them to some kind of action. Then discuss the results of that action. Let them know there is a problem for them to solve.

## Style of Leadership

Their leadership style is characterized as a practical and concrete, action-oriented approach. They are masterfully pragmatic in difficult and tense situations and are more energized by emergent circumstances than day-to-day routines. They pride themselves on giving expedient and efficient responses to situations. Their passion for precision and focus often means that they like to "roll up their sleeves" and help get the job done; in fact, they would rather show you than talk about how to achieve certain tasks. They are often flexible as leaders until they are forced to deal with emotional situations. They are often more concerned about precision, immediate action, and competence in a given situation than they are with either planning or developing learning partnerships with others that require extended interpersonal effort. Their strength as action-oriented leaders becomes a weakness when they are perceived as shortsighted and disinterested in the interpersonal needs of followers and associates.

## Creative Expression

Their creativity is engaged in solving problems about ways to integrate new frames of reference. Handy, practical, and efficient, they won't waste time on things that can be better handled by others. Instead, they move on to what seems incongruent to rectify sticky situations. Their proposals sometimes push the boundaries of what is expected, and they delight in innovations that reshape current ways of doing things or thinking about things. They use their keen sense of observation to notice what is going right and what is going wrong in accordance to their closely held principles and knowledge. They are the tricksters who surprise others with their probing questions and agility in combining things in new and refreshing ways.

## On a Team

### Naturally Bring to a Team

⇨ Focus more on the task to be completed than on the individuals doing the work; their relationships are about taking action
⇨ Good at helping people with problem solving
⇨ Talented at troubleshooting using tools and instruments
⇨ Resourceful—using the resources at hand
⇨ Analytical, observational, and skilled at using frameworks for solving problems

### Teamwork Style

⇨ Want to make a contribution; thrive on challenging situations
⇨ Prefer action-driven problem solving; are egalitarian, pragmatic, expedient, directive
⇨ Do whatever is necessary to get the job done

### Potential Blind Spots

⇨ May be uncomfortable with "social stuff" or talking through interpersonal problems
⇨ May miss implications of their actions
⇨ May appear to ignore authority to remain autonomous
⇨ Tend to enjoy personal achievement more than group or team accomplishments

### To Help Them Succeed

⇨ Allow autonomy and individual contributions
⇨ Provide opportunities to solve specific, concrete problems, especially "hands-on" contributions
⇨ Help them check their impulses against the long-range plan
⇨ Avoid direct confrontation; it may result in their insistence on what they think is appropriate and what they want

8

## Dealing with Your Stress

Being gifted at solving practical and factual problems, you can easily develop anxiety when there are no such problems to solve, when others prevent you from immediately doing so, or when you witness inefficient attempts to solve something, or when you have to wait for others to solve the obvious. Tending to be your own worst critic, you find it most distressing when you have not behaved efficiently in your work and have to redo and/or rework things. Within all organizations, you have very little patience for incompetence, inefficiency, and illogical and unreasonable behaviors. You can experience much stress when you become bored—boredom that is defined as not only the lack of physical activity but a lack of cognitive and sensory stimulation as well. Often such a bored state can give rise to anxiety, which in turn can feed a mood of restlessness and discontent.

### Prescriptions for Stress

☞ Consider engaging in recreational activities beyond just sports (whether as spectator or participant) such as board games, darts, nature trail hiking, camping, snorkeling, photography.

☞ Have regular experiences with various body-work modalities and treatments, such as massage, reflexology, acupressure, or shiatsu.

☞ Recenter and refuel with any and all forms of humor; laugh and play daily.

☞ Find frequent opportunities to engage with select close friends or family for storytelling and sharing the sensory pleasures of good food, drink, and ambiance.

## How You Learn

To get excited about learning, you need to actively solve problems. You like to observe how things work and to truly understand a situation. Sometimes that means taking something apart and making discoveries. You like learning how to use tools, but you need to be independent and learn by doing rather than just reading. You want to find all the angles, so you like to question and challenge. If you are given the framework or the model, you'll find the best approach. You enjoy getting hunches about how things work and applying the models to solve problems.

## For Your Career Mastery

You will engage in an inward tough-minded analysis of the fit with current environment while considering other available options that might meet your need to solve practical problems and to be independent. You will connect with a focal group of contacts but may miss opportunities that come from larger-scale efforts to connect with others who might have helpful information or valuable contacts. Your responsiveness to the needs of the moment and your realistic approach to problems are pluses. When connecting with others, be sure to speak up, sell yourself, and to show your ability to be a team player. You may use the Internet or other database resources to good effect when gathering information about career positions. Your need for things to be fun or to keep your options open may prevent you from doing the less exciting parts of a career search. You will critically weigh the pros and cons of career/job options but may not consider the impact of decisions on your personal life and significant others and whether or not they will like a job, even if it seems to be a good fit. You may have short-term tangible goals, but no long-term plan, and you may postpone decisions.

### Challenge Yourself

Reach out and connect with others, clarify what is truly important to you, clarify longer-term goals, set deadlines for making decisions, decide, and follow through.

## Reminders for Personal Growth

Find a place where you can use your creative problem solving and adaptiveness without rules and regulations. Find your own path to learning. Know people who explore alternate ideas and meanings. Travel to distant lands. Maintain a comfortable, fun, natural working and living environment. Build in daily alone time, outdoors time, and tool time. Use a structured way to meet and interact with new people who share your values. Spend some time learning about your values. Successful interpersonal relationships require negotiating to the other person's pace and attitudes. With others, consider three ways they could perceive the ethics and intentions of your words and actions. Have a set of tools to activate and use your intuitions, to think outside the box, and to cultivate strategy over mysticism. Realize that sometimes you can vary things a lot and have a powerful impact. Notice that not everything or everyone responds to a problem-solving approach. Remember that the uncertainty of tomorrow is a clear reason to play it smart today. Trust your hunches.

9

**Understanding the ESFP**    Motivator Presenter™

Temperament: **Improviser**™ · Interaction Style: **Get-Things-Going**™ · Cognitive Processes: **Se, Fi, Te, Ni | Si, Fe, Ti, Ne**

## Snapshot

Theme is performance. They are warm, charming, and witty. They want to impact and help others, to evoke their enjoyment, and to stimulate them to act. They want to make a difference and do something meaningful. Often masterful at showmanship, entertaining, motivating, and presenting, they thrive on social interaction, joyful living, and the challenge of the unknown. They like helping people get what they want and need, facilitating them to get results.

## When Solving Problems

They generally make decisions quickly about what action to take but may vary the decision when new options for action are seen. They take in a lot of rich detail, noticing minimal nonverbal cues. They are responsive to the needs of the immediate situation, especially regarding people and their reactions. They base decisions on what is important in relation to what is happening in the immediate external world. They automatically attend to what will make people satisfied and seek to help them do what they want to do. To influence them, join them in figuring out what else to try and show how it is relevant and important. Let them know what you like and want and how they can help.

## Style of Leadership

Their leadership style is characterized by enjoyment of relationships and sensory experiences. They tend to be realistic in outlook and in attending to the activities and tasks necessary as a leader. Masterful at building team support and encouraging others to perform, they are energetic and easy to be with, often lively and appreciative of others. Making a good impression is important to them, so they may go out of their way to accommodate the needs of others. They like to facilitate practical, concrete action plans among harmonious and cooperative team members. They seek out tangible results concurrent with being playful and having fun in their work. More interested in a comfortable and pleasant interaction in the present moment than in managing conflict and discord to explore new ideas and possibilities, their strengths, when overplayed, become weaknesses in settings where long-term planning and analytical problem solving must be demonstrated as essential leadership attributes.

## Creative Expression

Their creativity is sparked by making things fun and exciting in impactful and personal ways. Involving others' hearts and bodies triggers their actions. They willingly take risks to spark and impress people with delight and awe. Personal worth is important to them, so their creations reflect this. They possess a sense of adventure and want to be included to help make things happen. Continually checking their values against what they perceive, their creativity is expressive and sensitive to the needs others have for being considered worthy. Their best creative work is done when they have the freedom to act without restraint and have room for fun and spontaneity.

## On a Team

### Naturally Bring to a Team

⇨ Warm and friendly, their relationships are about caring, sharing experiences and having fun together
⇨ Good at getting people to cooperate with them; they like helping people get what they want and need
⇨ Easy to get along with; they can be counted on to get people working together
⇨ Provide a keen sense of reality, so are able to spot trouble early
⇨ At their best when responding to a crisis, they are tactical and maneuver quickly
⇨ Genuinely care, are generous, and are willing to help

### Teamwork Style

⇨ Easygoing, yet pragmatic and expedient
⇨ Will do whatever is necessary to get the job done with the least possible effort
⇨ Tend to get a process going and summarize decisions as they occur
⇨ Get others enthused and energized around the project

### Potential Blind Spots

⇨ May misread others' intentions and personalize events
⇨ Tend to be uninterested in abstractions unless they are relevant
⇨ May ignore interpersonal problems to avoid negativity
⇨ Might not implement an approach suggested by someone else

### To Help Them Succeed

⇨ Allow them autonomy and freedom from routine and hierarchy
⇨ Don't tell them they can't do something
⇨ Present potential roadblocks and problems as challenges
⇨ Provide choices, opportunities, flexibility, and a chance to work with people

10

Motivator Presenter™  **Being an ESFP**

Temperament: **Improviser**™ · Interaction Style: **Get-Things-Going**™ · Cognitive Processes: **Se, Fi, Te, Ni | Si, Fe, Ti, Ne**

## Dealing with Your Stress

Find yourself stressed when people don't respond to you with a sense of immediacy and action. Taking pride in your natural powers of persuasion, you can become unsettled and dismayed when your presentation isn't listened to and responded to both positively and quickly. Based on your natural predisposition to get involved and help others, you can easily find yourself double-booked and overextended. You can become offended when others criticize you for your ability to keep things light and/or make light of things. Often your upbeat jovial attitude and postures can be received with rejection and/or criticism by coworkers and colleagues. Such interpersonal tensions are sources of much frustration. These negative emotions can escalate, especially when the organizational "mood" is perceived as becoming "dry," cautious, and concerned.

### Prescriptions for Stress

☞ Learn to ask for and accept help with managing details, deadlines, and paperwork in any and all areas of life.

☞ Experiment with structured time for rest and relaxation processes. The use of audio- and/or videotapes for guided relaxation and centering exercises may be a valuable resource to employ.

☞ Develop and strengthen the ability to set healthy boundaries and speak assertively through classes, tapes, or one-on-one coaching.

☞ Establish and maintain a fitness program that includes opportunities to work up a good sweat, for example, a spinning class or step aerobics.

## How You Learn

You love to learn, especially about people. You want to be engaged in your learning through stimulating action and personal involvement. Since you love opening up people to possibilities, you want an opportunity to immediately share the possibilities when you see them. It also helps if there is a little drama, flair, and style to the teaching. You need to feel that the teacher genuinely cares. You need to have enough of a grasp of a subject so you can make sense of it. Then you'll learn all you need as long as you can see what you are going to do with what you learn.

## For Your Career Mastery

You will move quickly to take advantage of currently available career options that offer a friendly environment where you can meet and help others. You will actively network with others and draw on past connections. You may miss opportunities that come from turning inward to explore the long-term implications of career actions. Your energy, practicality, love of life, and flexibility are pluses. When connecting with others, you will sell yourself well and come across as a team player, but be sure to communicate your serious side, your task skills as well as your people skills, and be sure to let others talk during interviews. Resist the urge to take stopgap jobs that are immediately available. You are excellent at gathering information through talking to others who have experience but may not consider unusual job options. You will weigh the impact of decisions on your personal life and significant others but may not look in a tough-minded way at the pros, and especially the cons, of any given option. You may weigh what others want too heavily. You have short-term tangible goals but may not have a long-term plan. You may have difficulty following through on plans that are made.

### Challenge Yourself

Look beyond the known, develop a long-term career plan, consider the long-term potential of any given job, and follow through on decisions and commitments.

## Reminders for Personal Growth

Your ability to do basically anything in life moderately well is among your most impressive abilities. Do something good with your gift of genuine feeling by taking actions to help people. Always keep exploring, expanding your horizons, and trying out ideas to act on. If you are unhappy, then your life lacks balance. Cultivate three friends who are different from you because the people you have fun with can't help you grow. Sometimes it is best to let sleeping dogs lie. When people are avoiding or delaying an action, try to understand why before giving suggestions or helping them make a change. Let go of past injustices by keeping and sharing what you have learned. Remember to care deeply about your own well-being and happiness as well as the desires of other people. Part of being selfish is not seeing the selfishness. It is important to check your imagination and perceptions by thinking about others' perspectives. Notice that real sophistication and substance are often complex, quiet, and hidden.

11

Temperament: **Improviser**™ · Interaction Style: **Behind-the-Scenes**™ · Cognitive Processes: **Fi, Se, Ni, Te** | **Fe, Si, Ne, Ti**

## Snapshot

Theme is composing, using whatever is at hand to get a harmonious, aesthetic result. Their talents lie in combining, varying, and improvising, frequently in the arts but also in business and elsewhere. With their senses keenly tuned in, they become totally absorbed in the action of the moment, finding just what fits the situation or the composition. They thrive on having the freedom to vary what they do until they get just the right effect. They take action to help others and demonstrate values and are kind and sensitive to the suffering of others.

## When Solving Problems

They seem to vacillate between slow decisions and quick action. They constantly check against their values and tend to adjust their actions as the situation changes to keep true to what is important. This can look like constantly changing their minds, especially if no immediate action is taken on an earlier decision. They tend to base actions on what is happening in the immediate external world that is relevant and try to stick with what's important and what will make something better. They get a strong sense of what is needed and try various approaches until the desired result is achieved. To influence them, acknowledge what is important to them and to others in a mutually beneficial way. Show how it will get the desired result.

## Style of Leadership

Their leadership style is characterized as trusting, pragmatic, and flexible. Cooperation, loyalty, and a focus on individual needs are the hallmark qualities of their approach to leadership challenges. They are masterful in gaining cooperation from others and in finding a practical concrete solution to whatever issue confronts them. Confident in areas where they have had extensive experience, they are likely to show initiative with a select few and build a close knit team of loyal associates. They influence through doing rather than telling and are guided in their actions by the values of pragmatic cooperation. They adapt quickly and quietly, making the changes necessary to work under new conditions. They are more likely to become absorbed with the events of the present and the practical action required to address whatever situation is in front of them than in being strategic, making a plan, or competing for resources. Their strengths, if overplayed, become a weakness in environments where social networks, long-range planning, and demonstrated analytical analysis are prized qualities.

## Creative Expression

Their creativity comes from a deeply held value around what is *really* important and then moves forward in quiet ways to instigate a calculated risk for change. The information about options often comes from clues in the surrounding environment. Always on the lookout for evidence of how things in the external environment are aligned to their personally held values, they creatively work with people behind the scenes to bring about a resolution to challenging, noticeable situations. Heartfelt in approach, their creativity is profound in its gentle persuasion of others or its tasteful combinations of tangible elements to represent inner harmony and peace for others to admire and engage with.

## On a Team

### Naturally Bring to a Team

- Humane and easygoing; their relationships are about camaraderie and having fun interacting
- Resourceful and creative, with a unique gift of compromising to get quality results
- Great at getting others to work together
- Talented at creatively solving immediate and concrete problems
- Hardworking; often prepared with researched data

### Teamwork Style

- Action oriented, pragmatic, and expedient
- Good at gently persuading others to get the job done
- Approach problem solving by listening to ideas, getting support, and persuading others
- Judge others based on their actions
- Give information to prompt action rather than directives

### Potential Blind Spots

- May ignore systems, policies, and procedures to achieve whatever needs to be done
- May have a passive response to anger or tension that may become withdrawal from the team
- May lose track of time when absorbed in the creative moment

### To Help Them Succeed

- Provide an environment with opportunities, choices, flexibility, and a few familiar and friendly people
- Present a positive, harmonious work environment
- Recognize and compliment soon after an accomplishment

12

Producer Composer™  **Being an ISFP**

Temperament: **Improviser**™ · Interaction Style: **Behind-the-Scenes**™ · Cognitive Processes: **Fi, Se, Ni, Te | Fe, Si, Ne, Ti**

## Dealing with Your Stress

You experience stress when your loyalty to those you're committed to and your own creative energies are at odds. Feeling pulled in opposing directions can result in a sense of becoming burdened and restricted. When you are unable to achieve a natural-born goal of balancing freedoms with connections to others, you can find yourself discouraged, drained, and critical of yourself and others. When engaged in your creative processes, you can easily lose track of time, budgetary constraints, physical boundaries and such. Often you are stressed when your creative efforts require structured follow-through and detailed maintenance. By defining yourself through your actions, being results oriented and always engaged in the moment, you can find it difficult to cope with a guarded, detailed, slowly paced approach. Chronic stress and burnout often leads to self-neglect in the form of poor or inadequate self-care, including taking unnecessary risks.

### Prescriptions for Stress

☞ Incorporate any and all forms of relaxation training and breathwork through classes, tapes, books.
☞ Update assertive behavior skills through any preferred means.
☞ Achieve a work-life balance by setting realistic limits for time, energy, and money for projects and people.
☞ Ask for and accept assistance with details and deadlines in all contexts.

## How You Learn

You're most interested in sticking with what's important and not just learning because it's required. You like learning that helps you take advantage of opportunities. It's fun to be able to pull things together and use your learning for creative problem solving. You enjoy building relationships, and having a relationship with your fellow learners as well as the teacher is important. You have your own personal style and need to be true to yourself. Sometimes you play against the expectations of others just for the learning and the experience that come from it.

## For Your Career Mastery

You quietly reflect on how well the current environment fits with your personal values while considering other available options that might meet your needs to have tangible impact and to help others. You connect with a focal group of contacts but may miss opportunities that come from larger-scale efforts to connect with others who might have helpful information or valuable contacts. Your willingness to be a team player, hands-on skills, and adaptability are pluses. When connecting with others, be sure to speak up, to sell your very real accomplishments, and to show your task as well as your people skills. Sensitivity to rejection may get in the way of your reaching out. You may use the Internet or other database resources to good effect when gathering information about career positions. You may not consider unusual job options, or fail to look at the long-term consequences of a short-term job decision. You will weigh the impact of decisions on your personal life and significant others but may not look in a tough-minded way at the pros, and especially the cons, of any given option. You may weigh what others want too heavily. You may have short-term tangible goals but no long-term plan and may postpone decisions.

### Challenge Yourself

Reach out to others, sell your strengths and accomplishments, clarify longer-term goals, set deadlines for making decisions, decide, and follow through.

## Reminders for Personal Growth

Surround yourself with people who recognize and support your talents and your originality. Be captain of your own ship and explore places beyond your sphere of life. Give yourself permission to follow the educational path best for you. Be careful people don't get the wrong idea when you behave like their friend. When giving suggestions, let people know whether or not you can really be involved. You will be happier and freer if you address some of the problems in your environment instead of living with them. Notice that silence doesn't count as communication. If you're not doing something for your life, then what are you doing? Do until your heart is content. Find ways to be rewarded without losing your ethics—imagine who you can help with your success! Use all your natural skills. Continually push your limits through new knowledge. Build up a tolerance to people who annoy you. Too simple a life stifles opportunities. Find three ways to experience the freedom that a structure can provide.

13

## Snapshot

Theme is supervising, with an eye to the traditions and regulations of the group. They are responsible, hardworking, efficient and interested in ensuring that standards are met, resources conserved, and consequences delivered. Their talents lie in bringing order, structure, and completion. They want to keep order so the organization, group, family, or culture will be preserved. They thrive on organizing and following through with commitments and teaching others how to be successful.

## When Solving Problems

They make task decisions quickly, but may make life decisions slowly if they have no conventional examples to follow. They pay attention to concrete facts and compare them to a large internal data bank of life experiences and stored information, as well as external rules and standards. They like lots of organized information when something new is being considered. Decisions are usually based on criteria for keeping order and completing tasks and the responsible thing to do. To influence them, give them organized, factual information, preferably in writing, early in the decision process. Then suggest how all of it connects to their experiences.

## Style of Leadership

Their leadership style is characterized by being a decisively organized, methodical implementor of plans, who is focused on targeted outcomes. Known for their ability to communicate well-defined tasks and realistic expectations for almost all activity, they are often masterful at structuring and pragmatically acting to get things done. As group leaders, they prepare step-by-step analysis that provides a clear, efficient plan of action to achieved stated goals. More concerned with stability and logical exactness than developing relationships through rapport building or developing strategic initiatives, their strengths, when overplayed can derail their leadership efforts, producing compliance rather than commitment from followers and associates.

## Creative Expression

Their creativity is sparked when perceived opportunities for greater order, teamwork, and accomplishment become obvious. When standards, structures, and tasks are missing, they create them and lead others to fit with the program. Confident that people and events can be controlled and comfortable about leading others to attain a goal, they impose realistic and measured procedures with an eye to improving access to critical data and correcting functioning to improve upon what already exists. Persevering, tenacious, and results driven, their creative urge is to engage others to execute a practical solution that exceeds what others have done, to go one better in demonstrable ways.

## On a Team

### Naturally Bring to a Team

➪ Responsible and helpful; their relationships are about showing caring and concern by providing structure
➪ Quickly see the right way to do tasks, focus on planning and timely completion
➪ Will establish procedures and activities that provide team members with a sense of belonging
➪ Committed to and responsible for the task—steady, dependable, and predictable workers
➪ Cooperative team players

### Teamwork Style

➪ Make sure things run smoothly by defining purposes and issues, planning, and attending to logistics
➪ Lead in areas that require a responsible, results-oriented approach
➪ Expect others to follow rules and procedures
➪ Relate to others in a direct manner, encouraging cooperative teamwork and motivating for quality performance

### Potential Blind Spots

➪ May be quick to tell others what they should or should not do
➪ May get bogged down by ambiguous situations
➪ May make others feel put down by their detailed instructions and strong need for control
➪ Often expect others to be more like them

### To Help Them Succeed

➪ Provide stability and time-tested practices and procedures
➪ Give specific examples and comparisons to make theories and abstractions work better for them
➪ Be prepared: have a time-and-task focus, have agendas and clearly defined outcomes, and follow the agreed-upon plan

Implementor Supervisor™     **Being an ESTJ**

Temperament: **Stabilizer**™ · Interaction Style: **In-Charge**™ · Cognitive Processes: **Te, Si, Ne, Fi | Ti, Se, Ni, Fe**

## Dealing with Your Stress

You experience much stress when you witness others within the system not being responsible, by your definition. You have a strong positive regard for the organization's hierarchy and clearly established lines of authority. When others disrespect, cross over, and attempt to break established chains of command, you tend to respond to such violations with anger and criticism. With the high value you place on belonging to the right group(s) in the right way, the lack of such membership can be profoundly stressful. Left uncorrected, this can become a significant source of depression. Organizationally, you can find it most unsettling when there aren't any (or enough) "measurable markers" indicating progress and current status. The lack of such markers can bring on a sense of losing control and that nothing is really being accomplished. Since you abhor inefficiency, you find waste and misuse of any resources completely unacceptable and even a danger to the system.

### Prescriptions for Stress

☞ Try any and all forms of physical activity, whether individually or with others. This can range anywhere from participating in the offerings of a gym to starting a neighborhood walkers club.

☞ Be involved in structured, routine, membership oriented leisure activities, such as a bowling league, golf group, dance classes, quilting club, ski group, or theater-goers club.

☞ Learn and practice empathic listening skills.

☞ Ask for assistance when needed and accept help when it's offered.

## How You Learn

You really like to educate yourself, and you seek out the necessary learning experiences. Learning helps you bring order to chaotic situations, be well-balanced, and formulate the steps to success. You approach learning with your usual industrious, work-hard attitude, but you do like to balance work with play. You have a philosophy of life and learn best when you can connect your wealth of life experiences to what you are learning. You apply your own high standards of economy and quality to your learning experiences, just like you do in the rest of your life.

## For Your Career Mastery

You will make plans and move decisively to make career changes or to find an environment that will meet your need to be responsible, busy, and effective. You actively network with others and draw on past connections. You may miss opportunities that come from turning inward to explore long-term potential of a job or long-term values. Your active ability to get things done, your stability, and your realism are pluses. When connecting with others, you will demonstrate your competence through describing details of experiences and accomplishments. Be sure to communicate your people skills as well as your task skills and to build rapport with others when talking about business. You will naturally talk to others and gather just enough factual information to make a career decision. Resist the tendency to rely too much on previous job definitions in considering what future positions would be a good fit. You will logically weigh the pros and cons of career/job options, but may forget to consider the impact of decisions on your personal life and significant others, and what is truly important to them. You are good at setting goals and following through. Remember that many good opportunities come through events/interactions that aren't planned.

### Challenge Yourself

Consider long-term goals and outlook for careers/jobs, gather information, do not rush decisions, show your people skills, and find ways to consider unusual options.

## Reminders for Personal Growth

Remember that navigating "the system" for others' success is one of your greatest strengths. Accept that the only constant is change. You can be a responsible adult in many ways—not all of them are traditional, and it's okay that not all of them will work for you. Remind yourself to give people privacy. Relationships will be better if you refrain from saying "I told you so" when the consequences you predicted come to pass. When the values of others or society disturb you, consider the broader enduring principles you share. When something's irregular, pointedly ask if or how the situation is an exception. It's okay to be a little cheesy and have fun. If you want people to support you, then take the time to get to know and support them as the unique human beings that they are. In important situations, check three times to make sure you are following in the spirit as well as the letter of your beliefs. An official personal guide in life can be a good thing, so choose wisely.

15

**Understanding the ISTJ** Planner Inspector™

Temperament: **Stabilizer**™ · Interaction Style: **Chart-the-Course**™ · Cognitive Processes: **Si, Te, Fi, Ne | Se, Ti, Fe, Ni**

## Snapshot

Theme is planning and monitoring, ensuring predictable quality. Thorough, systematic, and careful, they see discrepancies, omissions, and pitfalls. Their talents lie in administrating and regulating. Dependable, realistic, and sensible, they want to conserve the resources of the organization, group, family, or culture and persevere toward that goal. They thrive on planning ahead and being prepared. They like helping others through their roles as parent, supervisor, teammate, and community volunteer.

## When Solving Problems

They decide quickly when they believe they understand the situation. When the situation is unfamiliar, they seek first to relate it to their previous experience, then make a cautious decision. Once a decision is made, it is not easily changed unless shown to be impractical. They like concrete facts more than hypothetical implications. They usually base their decisions on keeping order and completing tasks. To be influenced, they need lots of information to compare to their large data bank of life experiences and stored information. Give them factual information, in writing, early in the decision-making process. Then leave them alone to plan and reflect so they can determine the necessary logistical preparations.

## Style of Leadership

Their leadership style is characterized as persistent, logical, and structured, with a focus on concrete and pragmatic action. Known for an attitude of "stick-to-itiveness" and loyalty, they confidently direct action toward stated outcomes. As leaders, they tend to be highly selective about their interpersonal disclosures and about the roles they take on, preferring those whom they know well and their own areas of expertise. Often more concerned about getting the job done than with making a good impression, their strength that leads to productivity may become a major derailment factor in their success if they are perceived as authoritarian, unempathetic, and disrespectful of interpersonal processes.

## Creative Expression

Their creativity plans, orders, and sequences procedures in service of accomplishing a goal. Personal standards are applied to measure effectiveness and good use of resources. Motivated to have their systems running smoothly, their creativity is piqued when an opportunity for streamlining and establishing order is eminent. The goal for initiating a change is to find a tangible way to align resources for maximum ease, comfort, and functioning. Clues for what to do are found in personal past experiences in meeting challenges, or in benchmarks others have provided. Their approach to creating is incremental, experimenting in small steps, and proceeds based on what has been tried and proven true.

## On a Team

### Naturally Bring to a Team

⇨ Highly organized, their relationships are about caring and responsibility
⇨ Focus on completing details of a task and meeting objectives in a no-nonsense way
⇨ Thorough, systematic and careful; they work with a steady energy to follow through on commitments
⇨ Feel responsible for others in the group

### Teamwork style

⇨ Expect others to follow the rules and procedures without question
⇨ Respect hierarchy and organizational structure
⇨ Plan and monitor in a thorough, systematic, and careful way
⇨ Tend to inspect work, comparing outcomes to a standard

### Potential Blind Spots

⇨ May focus on their responsibilities to the neglect of personal relationships
⇨ May be overly cautious, especially when roles are unclear
⇨ May sometimes be seen as too serious and task focused

### To Help Them Succeed

⇨ Provide opportunities for alone time, periods of time for reflection and planning
⇨ Anchor incentives in reality, making them tangible, tried, and proven
⇨ Present change in terms of usefulness or practicality
⇨ Acknowledge their attention to duty and exceptional use of quantitative and standardizing skills
⇨ Help them develop their interpersonal communication skills

16

Planner Inspector™　　Being an ISTJ

Temperament: **Stabilizer**™ · Interaction Style: **Chart-the-Course**™ · Cognitive Processes: **Si, Te, Fi, Ne | Se, Ti, Fe, Ni**

## Dealing with Your Stress

You find it most stressful to be in organizations where clear, detailed, concrete, and specific instructions and expectations are not articulated. Any ambiguity or arbitrary changes in one's prescribed duties and responsibilities can generate much tension, anxiety, and a defensive posture. Holding such a strong work ethic, coupled with your talents at logistical planning, you can often wear yourself out overworking and overdoing your duty. Fatigue and tiredness are often ignored as you push yourself to the outer limits of your stamina and endurance. Such choices can increase both your stress levels and your health risks. Your tireless efforts for the sake of the institution's preservation often go unappreciated, or worse yet, unnoticed. Such an awareness can generate resentment and frequently feed a mood of irritability. Believing that play and leisure time are to be earned by hard work, you can be easily frustrated and distressed when others aren't doing their job.

### Prescriptions for Stress

☞ Start a daily humor diet. Cut out a cartoon and post it at work, share a funny story or joke daily, subscribe to a "joke a day" e-mail group.
☞ Explore and develop structured leisure time for yourself and with others. Consider board games, puzzles, models, crafts, and handiwork.
☞ Start taking "your turn" now (today) for weekend getaways, season tickets for events, vacationing and touring, and an occasional splurge on purchasing something extra or "indulgent" for self.
☞ Schedule regular massage therapy sessions and experiment with other therapies such as acupressure or shiatsu.

## How You Learn

You take responsibility for your learning and are loyal to your role as a student. You want to be prepared and will plan how you are going to learn something. You want to get the work done first before you can relax. If a learning experience turns out to be harder than you thought, you will do the right thing and overcome the adversity of the experience by working hard at it. You like cultivating good qualities and will bear the burden of difficult learning experiences to accomplish that. It helps if the learning is well organized, where nothing is missing or out of sequence.

## For Your Career Mastery

You will thoroughly consider the sensibleness of career moves before taking action and will seek environments that meet your need to be planful, responsible, and task oriented. You will connect with a focal group of contacts, but may miss opportunities that come from larger-scale efforts to connect with others who might have helpful information or valuable contacts. Your dependability and responsible style are pluses. When connecting with others, be sure to sell yourself and to show your people skills as well as your task skills. You are excellent at gathering factual information about career positions and may use the Internet or other database resources to good effect. You may fail to consider unusual job options or rely too much on a previous job definition in considering future positions. You will logically weigh the pros and cons of career options but may forget to consider impact of decisions on your personal life and significant others and whether or not you will like a job, even if it seems to be a good fit. You are good at setting goals and following through. Remember that many good opportunities come through events/interactions that aren't planned.

### Challenge Yourself

Reach out to others, take action, show your people skills, and find ways to consider options that don't seem to fit with past experiences.

## Reminders for Personal Growth

Find a place that appreciates your attention to responsibility while letting you care for yourself. You don't have to always please everyone. Remember that what you have found in your life is not what many others find in theirs. It is safer to take small incremental risks than a huge impulsive one and to do your homework and really use others' advice in making big decisions. Live with people who get you out in the world to have fun. Remember to kick off your shoes when it's time to relax. Remember, not everything needs a checklist. Practice naming and expressing your feelings. Seek volunteer experiences that engage your personal side and expand your identity. Try to learn three lessons from your children's successes or the younger generation. Sometimes your head will have to swim before your hard work can assure security. Stay well connected to friends. You can learn from conflict. Allow others to do things their own way or they will walk out of your life. Past a certain point, repetition does not count as experience.

17

Temperament: **Stabilizer**™ · Interaction Style: **Get-Things-Going**™ · Cognitive Processes: **Fe, Si, Ne, Ti | Fi, Se, Ni, Te**

## Snapshot

Theme is providing, ensuring that physical needs are met. Their talents lie in supporting others and supplying them with what they need. They are genuinely concerned about the welfare of others, making sure they are comfortable and involved. Use their sociability to nurture established institutions. Warm, considerate, thoughtful, friendly, they want to please and maintain harmonious relationships. They thrive on helping others and bringing people together.

## When Solving Problems

They often make quick decisions for the welfare of others. Task decisions are made quickly if direction and sequence are clear but may be changed if a new decision will be more helpful. They tend to research a great deal, seeking concrete facts to compare to their large data bank of personal experiences and stored information, especially about people. Their focus is on keeping harmony and considering how decisions will affect people they know and care about. They often take on too much and ignore their own needs. To influence them, give them information in person or verbally, especially about the impact on people and then give them time to reflect and analyze the situation.

## Style of Leadership

Their leadership style is characterized as personable and practical in efforts to help and support others. Their efforts are to produce predictable activities that promote caring and harmony. Often they are masterful at building cooperative relationships and maintaining group traditions or customs that enhance the "social glue" of a team. Often relentlessly attentive to the needs of others, they see their leadership as providing a service to promote higher levels of performance in others. More concerned with harmony and group cohesion than with strategic planning or envisioning the future, their strength can derail their leadership efforts when they fail to manage discontent and conflict effectively and fail to create opportunities for strategic considerations.

## Creative Expression

Their creativity engages others to connect in relevant ways. Working with others, for others, on behalf of others drives their energy to network and connect people with shared interests, aspirations, and experiences. Finding new people with common interests and rallying them to join together to work for the greater good is a driver for creative action. The welfare of others is paramount. Their creativity targets improving the human habitat so people can actively connect in lively conversation, solve problems, generate ideas, and reward results with esprit de corps within a communal effort. Their creativity comes to light when opportunities for harmony and fun in service of the community or team are perceived. They know the outcome of the friendly intercourse can positively impact and affirm others and motivate them to surpass past accomplishments to meet the demands of whatever situation they are in.

## On a Team

### Naturally Bring to a Team

⇨ Supportive of others; their relationships are about a genuine concern for the welfare of team members
⇨ Organize, prepare, and remember important events
⇨ Focus on harmony; they are often seen as a facilitator/caretaker on a team
⇨ Provide logistics, especially in service to others or to the organization

### Teamwork style

⇨ Organized; good at providing a sense of security and independence to others
⇨ Expect others to follow the rules and procedures
⇨ Intent on knowing others' needs and providing for them
⇨ Foster positive relationships using cooperation, enthusiasm, and consensus building
⇨ Softly authoritarian and decisive, give information to prompt rather than directing others' actions

### Potential Blind Spots

⇨ May avoid or smooth over conflict even when issues need to be addressed
⇨ May be overly sensitive to feedback and criticism
⇨ Are sometimes overloaded in an attempt to respond to the needs of others

### To Help Them Succeed

⇨ Comfort them with routine, and a secure, stable work environment
⇨ Provide appreciation and meaningful support for who they are and what they do
⇨ Give advance notice of change with information about the background and rationale for the change

18

Temperament: **Stabilizer**™ · Interaction Style: **Get-Things-Going**™ · Cognitive Processes: **Fe, Si, Ne, Ti | Fi, Se, Ni, Te**

## Dealing with Your Stress

You find yourself stressed when all the work (help) done to and for others doesn't get the recognition and appreciation you've earned and deserve. You can find it depressing when you're not actively involved in "doing" for others and not involved with what's going on within any system. Respecting and adhering to standard operating procedures, policies, and organizational hierarchies, you can be deeply offended and find it stressful to witness coworkers and colleagues behaving outside the norm. Here your generally warm, friendly, considerate manner can be overshadowed by a critical judgmental or dictatorial attitude. This can be further manifested as complaining about how bad things are, what others are doing wrong, and what should be happening. Often, this can become a vicious circle, for such behaviors can alienate, displease, and drive away the very relationships you are so hungry to care for and maintain.

### Prescriptions for Stress

☞ Try structured leisure time activities done independently—watercolor painting, sewing, gardening, woodworking, arts and crafts. It's critical to engage in these activities on your own, for this is a time for self only.

☞ Learn to set healthy limits, boundaries, and balancing commitments via classes, books, tapes, and so on.

☞ Learn to ask for and accept help.

☞ Develop assertive language skills via classes, tapes, books, coaching.

## How You Learn

You love learning anything that will help people accept and help each other. That kind of learning just comes naturally. You want to be in a learning environment where you can hear people and where concerns are voiced and needs accommodated. You truly admire the success of others, and hearing about those successes helps you learn. You think managing people is the most important part of the learning experience. If it's done well, you can learn. If not, then you'll try to provide others with what they need and keep the situation pleasant. You learn better if the instructor maintains a sense of continuity and remembers what's important.

## For Your Career Mastery

You will make plans and move decisively to make career changes or to find an environment that will meet your need to be responsible, be busy, and build good relationships. You will actively network with others and draw on past connections. You may miss opportunities that come from turning inward to explore long-term career direction or the long-term potential of a job. Your enthusiasm/warmth, sense of responsibility, and willingness to be a team player are pluses. When connecting with others, you will naturally give details of experiences and accomplishments. Be sure to communicate your task orientation in addition to showing your people skills, and to listen as well as talk in interviews. Don't let sensitivity to rejection get in the way of reaching out. You will naturally talk to others and gather just enough factual information to make a career decision. Resist the tendency to rely too much on previous job definitions in considering what future positions would be a good fit. You will weigh the impact of decisions on your personal life and significant others but may not look in a tough-minded way at the pros, and especially the cons, of any given option. You may weigh what others want too heavily. You are good at setting goals and following through. Remember that many good opportunities come through events/interactions that aren't planned.

### Challenge Yourself

Consider long-term goals and outlook for careers/jobs, gather information and don't rush decisions or take tough search experiences personally. Find ways to consider unusual options.

## Reminders for Personal Growth

Your gift of caring for other's needs is surpassed only by your gift for knowing their needs. Keep in mind that people are diverse, and it's okay if they feel a little odd. Consider that sometimes leaving people alone is the best way to help them mature. Interpersonal drama is not a good substitute for genuine love. Keep in mind that most other people simply cannot be as up front emotionally as you because they are concerned about the meaning of what they are doing. It's okay to be independent—you'll survive. It's okay to say no or "why don't you try first?" in response to others' demands—everyone will survive. Help people cultivate courage. Before committing, consider how grateful someone can be. Occasionally, helping hands hurt the most. Not everyone is at home with tradition. Overcoming adversity can be the highest measure of character. Try to leave room for people to pursue bright ideas that help others in new ways. Remind people that love is as love does.

19

Temperament: **Stabilizer**™ · Interaction Style: **Behind-the-Scenes**™ · Cognitive Processes: **Si, Fe, Ti, Ne | Se, Fi, Te, Ni**

## Snapshot

Theme is protecting and caretaking, ensuring their charges are safe from harm. Their talents lie in making sure everything is taken care of so others can succeed and accomplish their goals. Desiring to serve the needs of individuals, they often work long hours. Friendly, respectful, unassuming, they thrive on serving quietly without fanfare. They are devoted to doing whatever is necessary to ensure shelter and safety, warning about pitfalls and dangers and supporting along the way.

## When Solving Problems

They generally make slow, careful decisions that usually stick unless there is a negative impact on someone they care about. They like of information and filter it through a large data bank of life experiences and stored information, looking for what is familiar. They want concrete facts and to see how the decision will affect the people they know. They want to be supportive and make sure things go right. Sometimes decisions will be made "by the book" in a conventional way just to reach closure. To influence them, give them information early in the decision-making process, then leave them alone to analyze it. Show them how the decision will be helpful to people.

## Style of Leadership

Their leadership style is characterized as being focused on roles that are helpful and fulfill duties. They are seen as considerate, cooperative, and committed to tradition and conformity that promotes harmony. They prefer a "democratic" leadership process and are careful in seeking to influence others through relationships. They expect others to fulfill their roles thoughtfully and to support the work of other members of the team. Often more concerned about harmony than about dealing with conflict constructively, their strength, which promotes a sense of belonging, becomes a weakness as they may be perceived as unwilling to "fight" for what they want or to "stand up" to defend other members of the team.

## Creative Expression

Their creativity helps others in practical ways based on how things should look, feel, sound, taste, and smell. Others' verbal and nonverbal affirmations are their standards for initiating a change. The look on people's faces and their tones of voice tell them a lot about the right direction to go. Quiet, behind-the-scenes conversations provide them with opportunities to find facts and connect with individuals whose well-being is touched. Their creativity is engaged to anticipate and address every personal detail. Their confidence in using new approaches is summoned from a successful past experience. They are even more willing to engage in new activities with the trust, support, and approval from others. Their memories of when everything went right drives their often invisible, step-by-step approach to change.

## On a Team

### Naturally Bring to a Team

⇨ Support and respect of others; their relationships are about caring about people
⇨ Provide order and structure, attention to detail and stability
⇨ Kind and understanding; they focus on harmony and mutual support through teamwork and a sense of belonging
⇨ Dedicated to making the team work smoothly
⇨ Dependable record-keepers, focusing on facts and details

### Teamwork Style

⇨ Often lead reluctantly; they are conscientious, committed, and dedicated
⇨ Expect others to follow rules and procedures without unnecessary and uncalled for questions
⇨ Caring, rule oriented, and quiet; they have a non-threatening, encouraging, open style
⇨ Respectful of others' experiences and talents

### Potential Blind Spots

⇨ In an effort to satisfy everyone, may have a hard time sticking up for themselves and being assertive
⇨ Tend to be seen as slow, overly methodical decision makers
⇨ Have little tolerance for ambiguity
⇨ Often seen as serious and concerned and may over-prepare for the worst

### To Help Them Succeed

⇨ Avoid overloading to the point of causing stress
⇨ Give positive feedback and acknowledgement
⇨ Provide time alone to reflect and plan
⇨ Help them to see the positives in change

Protector Supporter™     **Being an ISFJ**

Temperament: **Stabilizer**™ · Interaction Style: **Behind-the-Scenes**™ · Cognitive Processes: **Si, Fe, Ti, Ne | Se, Fi, Te, Ni**

## 20

## Dealing with Your Stress

You tend to be stressed when there are too many unknowns or an unpredictable future, which can mean not being able to protect that and those you are responsible for. When such uncertainties are magnified, coupled with a focus on the worst-case scenario, you may react with excessive worrying. Left unchecked, your anxieties can begin to interfere with regular routines and daily functions. Ironically, such a stress reaction further impairs your own energies, efforts, and needs to serve, protect, and support. You often set few or no limits as to how long you will work on a project or program within any system. Quietly working long hours and going above and beyond the call of duty, you become easily susceptible to the effects of long-term stress, i.e. "burnout." You may find yourself being easily taken advantage of, taken for granted, and/or overused within the institution. This can develop into a quiet resentment and foster a prevailing mood of depression.

### Prescriptions for Stress

☞ Set up a healthier balance between your work and personal life. Attempt to get some needs met outside of your workplace in civic groups and organizations, service clubs, charities, and so on.

☞ Explore and discover one or two personal hobbies or leisure time activities.

☞ Learn to listen to your body's messages and respond quickly.

☞ Set up "minibreaks" throughout the workday for rest and refueling using stretching, yoga in a chair, focused breathing, a quick walk, a catnap, and so on.

## How You Learn

In your learning you like having an opportunity to notice what's needed and what's valuable, to know the ins and outs. You enjoy traditions and knowing what to expect. You want the purpose of your learning to be to help you work to protect the future. You prefer to learn in a caring, organized, and supportive environment. An opportunity to listen and remember helps you learn. You get exasperated when people ignore rules and don't get along. Being friendly and supportive is the best thing an instructor can do for you besides help you feel a sense of accomplishment.

## For Your Career Mastery

You will thoroughly consider the sensibleness of career moves before taking action and will seek environments that meet your need to be conscientious, organized, and to help others. You will connect with a focal group of contacts but may miss opportunities that come from larger-scale efforts to connect with others who might have helpful information or valuable contacts. Your stability, warmth, and willingness to be a team player are pluses. When connecting with others, be sure to sell your strong points and to communicate your task orientation in addition to your people skills. Sensitivity to rejection may keep you from reaching out. You are excellent at gathering factual information about career positions and may use the Internet or other database resources to good effect. You may fail to consider unusual job options or rely too much on previous job definitions in considering future positions. You will weigh the impact of decisions on your personal life and significant others, but may not look in a tough-minded way at the pros, and especially the cons, of any given option. You may weigh what others want too heavily. You are good at setting goals and follow through. Remember that many good opportunities come through events/interactions that aren't planned.

### Challenge Yourself

Reach out to others, sell yourself and your task skills, and find ways to consider unusual options that don't seem to fit with past experience.

## Reminders for Personal Growth

Your ability to hear and support others even at the cost of your own interests is among your greatest gifts and greatest burdens. It's okay to take pride in your accomplishments. Take comfort in the fact that most of history's greatest individuals succeeded quietly through patience, wisdom, and humility. Keep in mind that three minor commitments can often become more demanding than one major commitment. Join the philosophical conversation of life—that is, keep asking questions and you will discover a new quality to living. Similarly, there is no place like home, but cultivate those who help you go out and travel the road of life on your own. Practice saying what is important for you and for you alone. Drowning your sorrows in all work or all play pains the ones who really love you the most. Go on an adventure now and then. Most times, people need more challenging and more appropriate responsibilities to succeed. There's no harm in breaking rules every so often.

21

**Understanding the ENTJ**

Strategist Mobilizer™

Temperament: **Theorist**™ · Interaction Style: **In-Charge**™ · Cognitive Processes: **Te, Ni, Se, Fi | Ti, Ne, Si, Fe**

## Snapshot

Theme is directing and mobilizing. Their talents lie in developing policy, establishing plans, coordinating and sequencing events, and implementing strategy. They excel at directing others in reaching the goals dictated by their strong vision of the organization and thrive on marshaling forces to get plans put into action. Natural organization builders, they almost always find themselves taking charge in ineffective situations. They enjoy creating efficiently structured systems and setting priorities to achieve goals.

## When Solving Problems

They are distant, seemingly impersonal. They gather conceptual and factual information to make their vision happen and find what is motivating. They orient to the external world quickly and pick up information that helps them make simultaneous assessments of a multitude of data points. They easily make decisions based on the organization and implementation of their strategy. To influence their decisions, present a logical argument about long-range implications and effectiveness. Don't confuse their decisiveness with being inflexible. They will quickly reprioritize so as to not waste time on things that won't get desired results. They may need to build a new premise for their logic so let them think about it.

## Style of Leadership

Their leadership style is characterized as strategic oriented with a vision and direction that are planfully executed and problem focused. They tend to communicate urgency and the importance of relentless analytical critique to improve whatever is in front of them. As leaders, they often thrive on complex and demanding situations which motivate them to marshal their intellectual abilities to envision outcomes and plan both the tactics and strategies needed to reach a goal. Making a good impression is important to them but not so much so as to curtail a blunt, often demanding interpersonal style. Often seen as dominant and aggressive, they seek to influence through competence and commanding presence. More concerned with directing energy toward the long-term issues of an organization and developing the competencies needed to reach those goals, their strengths may derail their leadership efforts as others experience condescension and intolerance for views outside of their vision.

## Creative Expression

Their creativity is brought into action when a challenge to execute what may seem to be a mundane directive is perceived as a test of competence. They rise to the occasion to design and execute the ultimate strategy with elegance. Ambitious to do it better, faster, and more penetratingly than any others have ever done, their energy structures, organizes, and networks in unpredictably predictable ways to actualize the vision of besting the best and outsmarting the rest. All the while they know that this one involvement is one leg of a long-term overall plan. Able to leap tall buildings in a single bound, their creativity involves directing others to find the best way to maneuver resources for greater efficiency and enjoys mapping out a route and then leading others to the promised land.

## On a Team

### Naturally Bring to a Team

⇨ A team player if that's what it takes to get the job done; their relationships are about mutual autonomy
⇨ Develop policy, establish plans, coordinate events, and implement strategy
⇨ Take a systems view of decision making, strategically analyzing to solve problems
⇨ Marshal the forces and energize others to participate
⇨ Use integrative thinking and objective critiquing of decisions, plans, and data

### Teamwork style

⇨ Direct others to reach goals
⇨ Are results and action-oriented
⇨ Typically take charge and command
⇨ Focus on time and task, working toward achievement

### Potential Blind Spots

⇨ May not praise or give feedback as often as others need it; overlook the human element
⇨ Are quick to judge when others are seen as stupid or do not take responsibility for their actions
⇨ Might become impatient and too controlling, especially when in a hurry for action
⇨ May not recognize that limitations on a situation can slow progress toward an anticipated outcome

### To Help Them Succeed

⇨ Allow them autonomy and encourage them to allow others to be autonomous and independent
⇨ Provide recognition for achievements and competency from someone they judge competent
⇨ Give logical reasons and rationale for following prescribed procedures
⇨ Allow them the freedom to develop strategies

Strategist Mobilizer™                                   **Being an ENTJ**

Temperament: **Theorist**™ · Interaction Style: **In-Charge**™ · Cognitive Processes: **Te, Ni, Se, Fi | Ti, Ne, Si, Fe**

## Dealing with Your Stress

You tend to be greatly stressed when your marshaling of forces to manifest the long-range vision is resisted, thwarted, or derailed. Under pressure, your talent for multitasking can be overdone, resulting in overloading yourself and others. You can often be oblivious to how your behaviors are experienced as controlling by others. When such is pointed out, it can be received and interpreted as an issue of your own incompetence, for example, not having behaved well and been effective with others. This can often increase feelings of self-doubt and even fuel a sense of guilt. Lacking direct authority over time, money, people, material, and so on can mean not having enough power to manifest and implement your strategic vision. Limited in power and assessing that things are not and indeed may not be accomplished as envisioned and desired, you can start to take over, becoming dictatorial and demanding. As a natural-born efficiency expert, you are easily frustrated by inefficiently run systems of any kind.

### Prescriptions for Stress

☞ Experiment with any and all forms of inner work—meditation, guided imagery, and affirmations. Structure time for engaging in these processes and rotate as preferred among them.

☞ Consider a physical exercise program that is outside a formal gym or fitness center, such as cycling or jogging.

☞ Explore avocation opportunities available in teaching by any means—be a guest lecturer at local college, conduct seminars, and so on.

☞ Develop skills to set healthy limits and boundaries (that are in line with personal goals and visions) via classes, tapes, or coaching.

## How You Learn

Learning helps you marshal resources toward progress. You often find yourself being a leader, and you want to learn to better maximize talents—your own as well as the talents of others. You approach your learning as you do everything else—by forging partnerships. Your goal is to become more competent, and you view most of life as a learning experience. This helps you balance peace and conflict. You use your talent for coordinating to apply your learning to multiple projects, even during the learning experience itself. You really enjoy intuitive explorations. You often have a kind of predictive creativity that helps you know what is important to learn.

## For Your Career Mastery

You will make plans and move decisively to make career changes or to find an environment that will support your need to take charge and solve complex problems. You will draw on a wide variety of relationships and actively network with others. You may miss opportunities that come from turning inward to explore long-term values and what you personally care about. Your energy, ingenuity, and drive to get things done are pluses. When connecting with others, you will sell yourself with confidence, but be sure to show diplomacy and sensitivity to people issues and to listen as well as talk during interviews. You will naturally talk to others, and need just a hint of an exciting strategic option before making a decision. Resist the tendency to overlook key job facts in your desire to make a quick decision. You will logically weigh pros and cons of career/job options but may not consider the impact of decisions on your personal life and significant others. You are good at setting goals and following through. Remember that many good opportunities come through events that aren't planned.

### Challenge Yourself

Gather enough information and don't rush decisions. Gather facts about the actual requirements of a job, clarify what's truly important to you, and show your people skills and tact/diplomacy as you connect with others.

## Reminders for Personal Growth

Trust, develop, and share your intuitions—but don't scare away too many people. Mentoring and promoting promising people is one of your greatest abilities. When people seem disinterested in maximizing their potential, consider what strong beliefs are motivating them toward something else. Even if you rise to the top of something conventional, it's still conventional—and the source of life's demanding details. Do not underestimate your ability to handle the status quo when it strikes back against change. Consider that your objective style may leave others confident in you but wanting something more personal. Take the initiative to get close to the those who interest you. Develop and check your moral compass early and often. Allow yourself and others some time to just play with ideas. Time off does not mean extra time for more work. Try three things to maintain your health and build in time for family and friends. Notice that without a quiet space for yourself, you will feel like all weather and no sunshine.

23

**Understanding the INTJ**  Conceptualizer Director™

Temperament: **Theorist**™ · Interaction Style: **Chart-the-Course**™ · Cognitive Processes: **Ni, Te, Fi, Se | Ne, Ti, Fe, Si**

## Snapshot

Theme is strategizing, envisioning, and masterminding. Their talents lie in defining goals, creating detailed plans, and outlining contingencies. They devise strategy, give structure, establish complex plans to reach distant goals dictated by a strong vision of what is needed in the long run. Thrive on putting theories to work and are open to any and all ideas that can be integrated into the complex systems they seek to understand. They drive themselves hard to master what is needed to make progress toward goals.

## When Solving Problems

Strategic decisions come quickly as they compare new information to their abstract representations of the universe. Concrete, logistical decisions often frustrate them or go unmade. They gather lots of information to base decisions on the "how" and "why" in terms of effectiveness. Their focus is on future applications and progress. An impersonal approach is usually taken. To influence their decisions, present a logical argument about long-range implications, build a new premise for their logic, and give them time and space to see where it fits in their framework. They may need to reconceptualize their whole system if what you propose is too different from their vision.

## Style of Leadership

Their leadership style is characterized as strategic and systemic regarding results. They are analytical and tough-minded in service to the vision they have created. They are often masterful managers of complexity in implementing a plan that moves an organization toward a vision of the future. Their commitment to efficiency and effectiveness drives them to identify problems in any system that comes their way for review. Often more concerned about consistency of action, plans, and vision than communicating details and processes needed to realize a plan, they may be perceived as unyielding, "headstrong," overly analytical, and impersonal. Their strength as strategic organizers is underscored by a passion for competence, which may become a weakness when they fail to listen to different perspectives or develop relationships with all of the relevant parties.

## Creative Expression

Their creativity appears as if out of nowhere. Internal considerations of perfection in all things, and the systems that support its realization, can be best articulated in abstract models based on masses of valid data and observational studies from diverse fields of discipline that are synthesized to such a point that using the tool of language alone is inadequate. Their energy is constantly challenged to improve what exists. The primary locus of attention for them is internal and few others know what workings of mind, what somersaults of vision and symbols frolic within. They are motivated to initiate a change to help stay the course on the road to excellence. They create elegant representations of concise abstractions that can be made useful. Of this they are certain.

## On a Team

### Naturally Bring to a Team

⇨ Are integrative and strategic; their relationships are about achieving a goal
⇨ Analysis; seeing differences and creating categories
⇨ Put theories to work by mapping out feasible events, developing agendas, building models
⇨ Tirelessly drive toward the goal
⇨ Use systems thinking, using deductive reasoning to synthesize and organize ideas

### Teamwork Style

⇨ Direct by defining the goal, creating detailed plans, outlining contingencies, and devising strategies
⇨ Are devoted to accuracy and precision; they have high expectations of themselves and others
⇨ Carefully make decisions with a focus on goals and a vision
⇨ Prefer privacy and autonomy and time for reflective thinking

### Potential Blind Spots

⇨ May be oblivious to the effect of their responses on others
⇨ Might not give praise and/or feedback as often as others need it
⇨ May be reluctant to delegate, preferring to rely on their own capabilities
⇨ Seem to believe they can be competent at anything

### To Help Them Succeed

⇨ Allow them autonomy
⇨ Give them respect for thoughts and feelings, ideas and creativity
⇨ Provide opportunities for constant evaluation and re-evaluation to meet their need for high achievement and competency
⇨ Put them in a situation where they can devise and implement long-range strategies aimed at efficient and effective use of the organization's resources

24

Conceptualizer Director™     **Being an INTJ**

Temperament: **Theorist™** · Interaction Style: **Chart-the-Course™** · Cognitive Processes: **Ni, Te, Fi, Se | Ne, Ti, Fe, Si**

## Dealing with Your Stress

Naturally at ease with the theoretical, under pressure you may insist on detailed data collection. Often with a stern directing quality, you may have others collect, identify, inspect, and categorize minute data to the point of leaving no grain of sand unturned. Significantly distressed when you can't anticipate what's going to happen or when what you've envisioned doesn't manifest itself as planned, your message to yourself can be, "If I were only smarter (truly competent), I would have figured this out or anticipated it ahead of time." Stress that leads to questioning and doubting of self can result in a shutting down of personal interactions and even withdrawing from the scene/context. At times, the "opposite" reaction may be opted for, namely choosing to bulldoze your solutions on through. Trusting logic and reason, you can be quickly annoyed when others appear illogical, subjective, and unreasonable.

### Prescriptions for Stress

☞ Explore and incorporate grounding meditation practices into existing private time pursuits such as Mindfulness-Based Stress Reduction, walking meditations, and/or Tai-Chi.
☞ Upgrade and increase the level of humor, laughter, and play in all areas, particularly in context with others.
☞ Structure sensory-oriented activities into your leisure time interests such as painting, ceramics, photography, cooking, playing music, or singing.
☞ Develop empathic listening and speaking skills via tapes, books, coaching.

## How You Learn

Learning is all about progress. You have an intense drive for self-mastery. You want your learning to help you build a vision with very long-range strategizing. You seek learning experiences that help you maximize achievements toward goals and be on the leading edge. You like learning experiences that use your natural way of systems thinking, where you can maintain your independence and find a way to reconceptualize. Sometimes this takes some reflection time, but other times it's going on in the background during the learning experience as you see the reasons behind things.

## For Your Career Mastery

You will thoughtfully consider a number of strategic long-term career options before taking action and will seek environments that meet your need to be imaginative, independent, and productive. You will connect with a focal group of contacts but may miss opportunities that come from larger-scale efforts to connect with others who might have helpful information or valuable contacts. Your competence, insight, and analytical skills are pluses. When connecting with others, be sure to sell yourself and to show your people skills as well as your task skills. Don't let unrealistic expectations about a job or the need to have a well-considered strategy get in the way of taking action. You will naturally gather information through reading, and get excited about a new career idea but may fail to register key facts and details about a career option. You will logically weigh the pros and cons of career/job options but may forget to consider the impact of decisions on your personal life and significant others and whether or not you will like a job, even if it seems to be a good fit. You are good at setting goals but may need to narrow the focus on exciting possibilities to an explorable short list so practical action can be taken.

### Challenge Yourself

Reach out to others, show tact/diplomacy, tentatively narrow your options so you can really move into action, and gather facts/data about your options.

## Reminders for Personal Growth

Trust your unconscious to pace and catalyze your work and ideas. Create a space and time to be alone to focus creatively without mundane demands. Recruit people who believe in you and your ideas. Show other people your projects and get feedback to keep your vision realistic. Consider that there are always more choices. Learn "people tools" to change how you feel and understand whom to trust. If you allow someone to influence your heart then you will never be alone. Try to maintain at least three good friends. Find an environment with the tools and resources to build and test your ideas. A mentor is a good way to get ahead. You don't need to experiment with or push every relationship in order to learn. Collect the feeling or meaning of each of your experiences in life. Have as many kinds of experiences as possible. Treat others as more human than you treat yourself. Be ready to rethink what "success" means. Remember to give expression to your feelings.

25

**Understanding the ENTP**    Explorer Inventor™

Temperament: **Theorist**™ · Interaction Style: **Get-Things-Going**™ · Cognitive Processes: **Ne, Ti, Fe, Si | Ni, Te, Fi, Se**

## Snapshot

Theme is inventing, finding ingenious solutions to people and technical problems. Their talents lie in developing ideas into functional and innovative applications that are the first of their kind. They thrive on finding new ways to use theories to make systems more efficient and people better off. Hungry for new projects, they have faith in their ability to instantly come up with new approaches that will work. They are engineers of human relationships and systems as well as in the more scientific and technological domains.

## When Solving Problems

They are quick to infer and read a situation. They make decisions quickly in response to new information regarding the system or the potential for making a complex model accessible and usable. They are hesitant when no strategy exists or when relationships are at risk. They quickly gather conceptual information to sort into categories, set criteria, and move to a meta-position with principles about how to problem solve. Decisions are based first on new possibilities that will get the job done and then on theoretical accuracy. They like having multiple models to use as guiding principles. To influence them, give them new information, another idea, and other options that will lead to improvement. Be prepared for a devil's advocate argument.

## Style of Leadership

Their leadership style is characterized as competitive, cutting edge, and relentlessly assertive with questions and analysis. They tend to be enterprising and resourceful in whatever field they choose. As such, they push boundaries as independent problem solvers who are masterful originators of new ideas and possibilities. Seen as confident and energetic, they are massive consumers of information. Quick to analyze and critique situations, they are problem focused rather than people focused in their interactions. As leaders, they look for trends and underlying principles in situations and pursue understanding these with gusto. More concerned with the concepts, knowledge, and frameworks that confront them as leaders than the people and relationship dynamics around them, their strengths become a weakness when they ignore the emotional needs of their followers and associates.

## Creative Expression

Their creativity evokes change for everyone involved. The subject may be new ways of doing business, new systems for organizational effectiveness, or far-reaching notions of what might be done to improve efficiencies and outcomes. The challenge must be intellectual and test the competencies and knowledge bases of those in the immediate environment, including them. Their creative energy is sparked in lively conversation and debate. The changes they are likely to initiate are ones that challenge the individuals involved to move from the status quo to create the next status quo and so on.

## On a Team

### Naturally Bring to a Team

⇨ Inventive at finding solutions to people and technical problems; their relationships are about constant idea generation
⇨ Great at developing ideas into functional and innovative applications
⇨ Analysis, seeing differences and creating categories; they have a unique ability to multi-focus
⇨ Project oriented; are skilled at synthesis and design

### Teamwork style

⇨ Highly energized, they are adept at mobilizing others and bringing them together in an information-giving manner
⇨ Typically communicate the general outline of a vision, then let everyone follow their interests toward achieving the plan
⇨ Engineer the relationships and systems

### Potential Blind Spots

⇨ Given abstract random thinking, may miss concrete data
⇨ Might jump to strategizing before others are ready
⇨ Can have difficulty expressing feelings and emotions
⇨ Frequently are impatient with repetition and errors
⇨ May be oblivious to conventions and protocol

### To Help Them Succeed

⇨ Give them nonroutine environments that allow entrepreneurial explorations and creative approaches to problem solving
⇨ Give them the opportunity to share insights about life's possibilities and to achieve success with those ideas
⇨ Provide challenge and intellectual stimulation
⇨ Give them autonomy and opportunities to invent and improvise solutions to complex problems

26

Explorer Inventor™          **Being an ENTP**

Temperament: **Theorist™** · Interaction Style: **Get-Things-Going™** · Cognitive Processes: **Ne, Ti, Fe, Si | Ni, Te, Fi, Se**

## Dealing with Your Stress

Although masterful as a "thinker upper," you are stressed when asked to implement your ideas (become a "getter doner"). Organizationally, you can find yourself appearing weakened when placed in a manifesting mode. The reality of not knowing the steps to be taken, because of naturally lacking the right skill set, can leave you feeling ignorant and doubting. Having to strictly adhere to the focus and guidelines already in place can be very taxing and generate restlessness. Although you easily can and do give corrections and criticisms to others, you can be hypersensitive to criticism from others. This is particularly so when your competencies and knowledge are challenged. Such feedback, coming from a credible source, can be very unsettling and easily awaken your constant nemesis, the sleeping giant of self-doubt. Getting caught up in your intricate system of thoughts and flurry of ideas can easily get you, and keep you, stuck on their path.

### Prescriptions for Stress

☞ Investigate and develop various forms of relaxation training, including guided imagery practices and creative visualization.
☞ Experiment with some basic time-management strategies and develop a healthier, more grounded, "relationship" with time.
☞ Share personal interests and hobbies with significant others on a fairly regular basis.
☞ Learn to set healthy limits and boundaries via classes, coaching, or tapes.

## How You Learn

Learning is about being inventive, seeing patterns and connections that lead to prototypes, and getting projects launched. You're a lifelong learner, and you want to strategically formulate your success so you can learn from anything, anytime, anywhere. You really enjoy the creative process, and your best learning occurs when you get to share your insights about life's possibilities with others as they occur. The drama of give and take in a lively debate really helps you learn. You try to be diplomatic, but sometimes making a point in a discussion takes priority.

## For Your Career Mastery

You will move quickly and spontaneously on career options if an exciting new possibility arises or if there are new challenges and opportunities to be innovative. You will actively network with a wide variety of people to explore options. You may miss opportunities that come from turning inward to examine the long-term direction of your career. Your enthusiasm, ingenuity, and versatility are pluses. When connecting with others, you will sell yourself with confidence, but be sure to show sensitivity to people issues and your ability to follow through, and to listen as well as talk during interviews. You will get excited when talking to others about new career ideas but may need to narrow your strategic options to a concrete and explorable short list. You may fail to register key facts about career options. Resist the urge to get distracted or to take the first exciting option that comes along. You will logically weigh the pros and cons of career/job options but may forget to consider the impact of decisions on your personal life and significant others, and what is truly important to them. You will be responsive to opportunities but may have no long-term sense of direction. You may have trouble following through on a career search plan.

### Challenge Yourself

Develop a long-term career plan, be sensitive to interpersonal issues in search activities, and gather facts about job options. Set deadlines for making decisions, decide, and follow through.

## Reminders for Personal Growth

Find a place where your brainstorming and insights into possibilities are appreciated and given credit. Be nice and play fairly. In relationships, get feedback on how much the other person wants to do problem solving. Keep your humor. Practice diplomatically articulating your needs, values, and feelings. Focus on what you are most passionate about. When, and if, you play politics, recognize that being political isn't *the* way but *your* way. If you cannot pinpoint someone's strategy or principle, then recognize it as their belief. It's okay to have three jobs at once, just remember to sleep, taste, and breathe. Not everything can be successfully approached using a technique. There are many kinds of intelligence—some aren't cognitive and it's okay that not all of them can be yours. Promote the worth of others. Try to name three personal beliefs about major ideas you engage. Affect announces character, so pay attention to nonverbal cues. Recognize that failure can result from overpreparation as well as underpreparation. Practice giving and compassion.

27

**Understanding the INTP**  Designer Theorizer™

Temperament: **Theorist™** · Interaction Style: **Behind-the-Scenes™** · Cognitive Processes: **Ti, Ne, Si, Fe | Te, Ni, Se, Fi**

## Snapshot

Theme is designing and configuring. Their talents lie in grasping the underlying principles of something and defining its essential qualities. They seek to define precisely and bring coherence to systems based on the pattern of organization that is naturally there. They easily notice inconsistencies. They enjoy elegant theories and models for their own sake and for use in solving technical and human problems. Interested in theorizing, analyzing, and learning, they thrive on exploring, understanding, and explaining how the world works.

## When Solving Problems

They quickly decide on the accuracy of theories and frameworks, yet labor over accurate expression of ideas. They may avoid decisions regarding an action or establishing order and structure. They gather conceptual information to sort into categories and may not act until guiding principles are clear. Their focus is on the accuracy of a theory and clarity of a model. Logistical decisions are seen as trivial and either slighted or labored over. Interpersonal decisions are made to avoid disruption and to keep the peace. To influence them, give them new information presenting other workable options. Be sure there is internal consistency in your logic and be prepared for mutual critique and debate.

## Style of Leadership

Their leadership style is characterized as promoting autonomous problem solvers committed to the same general vision. Conceptual and analytical regarding systemic problems in a given situation, they are persistently critical. Masterful at developing competence and expertise in many fields, they enjoy solving complex problems so much that they may fail to delegate to others. They tend to believe that there is an underlying theory in all things—including human behavior—and build their understanding around their theory of choice. Often more concerned with theoretical and abstract purity than with practical tasks and encouraging those who must actualize the theory or vision, their strength for intellectual ingenuity can become a weakness if they are perceived as unconcerned about others' views or they seem to waste too much time analyzing competing propositions about a situation or event.

## Creative Expression

Their creativity is aroused when inconsistent theoretical frameworks of understanding are juxtaposed. Comparing how things are intended to work to how they actually do work is a captivating and intriguing puzzle. Taking

two or more models of thought and integrating them to reveal a more holistic and better-defined essence is personally fulfilling. While they muse alone or hypothesize with others in quiet dialogue about deeply considered conceptual and actual matches and mismatches, a third, fourth, or fifth potential emerges that seemingly better articulates a common seed for the models under consideration. Careful, focused thought is given to systemic integrity; examples of the uniqueness of each potential is logically counterbalanced using intellectual rigor until a new, simpler truth is unveiled. Inferences about the future consequences of subscribing to the new truth abound. Their energy is motivated to initiate a change when they observe inconsistency of thought and action.

## On a Team

### Naturally Bring to a Team

⇨ Bring clarity to defining problems; their relationships are about sharing expertise
⇨ Design and theorize; they often grasp underlying principles and define essential qualities
⇨ Analysis, pointing out differences and developing categories
⇨ Use wordsmithing to express exactly what they and others want to communicate
⇨ Focus on the principles of a project

### Teamwork Style

⇨ Engineer connections—help connect people with ideas and information as well as network people to people— usually around expertise
⇨ Communicate the general outline of a vision
⇨ Can provide autonomy and options, assuming others want it as much as they do

### Potential Blind Spots

⇨ Are impatient with errors, covering ground already covered, and other signs of inefficiency
⇨ May be seen as not caring or not being a team player when they detach to analyze, critique, and problem solve
⇨ Might avoid conflict too long, hoping it will go away
⇨ Can irritate team members by being too theoretical

### To Help Them Succeed

⇨ Provide them enough freedom to reflect on how things work, to generate ideas, see connections and patterns.
⇨ Provide them opportunities to direct their energy toward the acquisition of knowledge and competence.
⇨ Give them the logic, rationale, or proof behind standard operating procedures, conventions, and protocols.
⇨ Provide coaching in interpersonal skills.

## Dealing with Your Stress

You can be quickly stressed when you don't understand why something is going on, i.e., when you can't figure it out. Experiencing such an impasse not only gets you feeling stuck but can be interpreted as evidence that you are obviously not clever enough and/or don't know enough. Your first line of defense for anything is to take the appropriate time to analyze it and create a match between need and possibility. Interpersonal relations, especially when in conflict, are most stressing and can render a sense of powerlessness. Although possessing a sensitivity to others, you often lack the people skills needed to interact empathically and show your genuine caring. This can further inhibit your willingness to try, which further increases your feelings of inadequacy, which can cause you to withdraw further and so on. It can feel like trying to "get a handle" on fog. Designing and theorizing take precedence over logistical and tactical implementation. As a result, following through and "making it happen" can leave you feeling burdened and inadequate.

### Prescriptions for Stress

☞ Enjoy quality time with family and close friends; entertain at home.
☞ Join professional peer associations in order to renew knowledge, experience up-to-date training, and connect with current issues in the field.
☞ Set up a physical fitness program that involves an aerobic component.
☞ Develop and practice empathic communication strategies.

## How You Learn

Learning, like life, is about becoming an expert, knowing all there is to know about something. You like learning that helps you see new patterns and elegant connections, cross the artificial boundaries of thought, and activate the imagination. You even like to reflect on the process of thinking itself. Intellectual discussions where you can clarify and define concepts help you learn. Sometimes in those discussions, you detach from the situation to analyze. Then you come back with a discovery that helps make things clearer.

## For Your Career Mastery

You will quietly analyze the fit with your current environment while considering other strategic career options that might meet your need to be innovative, tough-minded, and independent. You will connect with a focal group of contacts but may miss opportunities that come from larger-scale efforts to connect with others who might have helpful information or valuable contacts. Your analytical skills, ingenuity, and creativity are pluses. When connecting with others, be sure to sell yourself, to build rapport, and to show your people skills as well as your critical thinking skills. Don't let unrealistic expectations for a job or the need to keep your options open get in the way of taking action. You will naturally gather information through reading and database exploration but may fail to register key facts about a career option. Will logically weigh the pros and cons of career/job options but may forget to consider the impact of decisions on your personal life and significant others and whether or not they will like a job, even if it seems to be a good fit. Although you may have multiple long-term options, you may have no long-term sense of direction and decision making may be postponed indefinitely.

### Challenge Yourself

Reach out and connect with others, clarify what is truly important to you, set concrete and tangible goals, set deadlines for making decisions, decide, and follow through.

## Reminders for Personal Growth

Find a comfortable collegial environment where you can play with and generate ideas. Locate your own interests. When explaining something, try to give three complete examples. Keep an eye on areas where thinking is rigid. If you express your vision and passion for the potential effect of your ideas and principles, then people will listen. Maintain openness to what is true socially or psychologically as well as conceptually. Try to maintain some links to enjoy life's pleasantries and, similarly, design a work area mostly free of mundane demands. Use multiple models for how to be diplomatic. Remember that when critiquing others' ideas, your questions about improvement will be received and acted on more often than your criticism. Acknowledge the physical world, your body, and the worth of anecdotal observation, or you may likely just float away. Find people who can turn your ideas into useful products that see daylight. Observe the observational processes of others. Enjoy the soothing sensation of walking barefoot in the grass. It's okay to express emotion.

Temperament: **Catalyst**™ · Interaction Style: **In-Charge**™ · Cognitive Processes: **Fe, Ni, Se, Ti | Fi, Ne, Si, Te**

## Snapshot

Theme is mentoring, leading people to achieve their potential and become more of who they are. Their talents lie in empathizing with profound interpersonal insight and in influencing others to learn, grow, and develop. They lead using their exceptional communication skills, enthusiasm, and warmth to gain cooperation toward meeting the ideals they hold for the individual or the organization. Catalysts who draw out the best in others, they thrive on empathic connections. Frequently, they are called on to help others with personal problems.

## When Solving Problems

Most decisions are made quickly except when they are not ready to make a decision. They gather personal information, including global impressions, feelings, and emotional tone. They need an opportunity to generate possibilities toward a plan. They will withdraw mentally to visualize the impact of new information on the people involved. They often base decisions on what is most fitting and suitable according to the values of the group. When a decision is based on strong values regarding what is right for themselves, they may be very hard to influence. Give them reflection time to sort through everything and readjust their vision. To influence them, show them how a decision will affect others or how boundaries have been breached.

## Style of Leadership

Their leadership style is characterized as expressively warm, supportive, and inclusive. They tend to position themselves as the spokesperson for the core values and ideals of an organization. Often they see their efforts as related to the development needs of others and in promoting understanding among individuals in a group. Masterful collaborators, they organize and facilitate action by building extensive networks and support for a given goal or mission. They often seek to make a good impression with others through building rapport and showing awareness of others' needs. More concerned with group harmony and group process than with a tactical project plan, their strength becomes a weakness when so overplayed in conflict situations that needed differences of opinion are not expressed and inefficiency is created because of too much effort in interpersonal processes.

## Creative Expression

Their creativity harmonizes people with goals for their own good. Based on a seeming instinct of what people need to do to get a job done well, they initiate changes to help people actualize their power in growth-oriented

socially acceptable ways. The goal is to help people thrive in their environments and be positively affirmed for their accomplishments. Natural networkers, they have energy that easily connects people to others, to processes, and to procedures that will help further their intent for a glowing personal success. With a coaching attitude, their creative energy surfaces when they are challenged to do their best to help others do *their* best.

## On a Team

### Naturally Bring to a Team
⇨ See potential in others; their relationships are about mentoring
⇨ Can be good at drawing out the best in others, providing team members with camaraderie, mutual support, and a commitment to the overall team effort
⇨ Talented at gaining consensus using collaboration and cooperation
⇨ Are catalysts who energize the team with enthusiasm and humor
⇨ Are tuned into organizational climate

### Teamwork style
⇨ Facilitate goal accomplishment through cooperation and considering all options
⇨ Use their communication skills, enthusiasm, and warmth to gain cooperation
⇨ Democratic and participative; they seek to mentor people to achieve their potential through coaching, encouragement, and by providing positive feedback
⇨ Encourage and honor diversity to utilize the resources of the team

### Potential Blind Spots
⇨ May get lost in relationships and become overburdened with the problems of others
⇨ Might become so involved coaching and assisting others that other tasks take a backseat
⇨ Tend to work in bursts of energy that may not coincide with the needs of the team
⇨ May have a hard time separating from their ideal and being objective

### To Help Them Succeed
⇨ Provide an open, harmonious, and sharing environment where they and others can self-disclose
⇨ Give them genuine, positive feedback—they value the approval of others
⇨ Provide opportunities for interaction
⇨ Frame the work in a context of some higher purpose

Envisioner Mentor™     **Being an ENFJ**

Temperament: **Catalyst™** · Interaction Style: **In-Charge™** · Cognitive Processes: **Fe, Ni, Se, Ti | Fi, Ne, Si, Te**

## Dealing with Your Stress

Fueled best by pure inspiration, you demonstrate an attitude of "chomping at the bit" when so empowered. But when the organization sets up roadblocks because you aren't being practical or logical, you react with disbelief and appear wounded. Your style wants and needs recognition and acknowledgment and you are often stressed by receiving little or no credit for your significant, unique contributions. Your uncanny gifts for being empathic can be both a blessing and a curse. One downside is a tendency to pick up and carry everyone's emotional issues and become unnecessarily and unconsciously over-burdened as a result. Finding it difficult to set limits and dissociate from everyone's personal demands of your time, energy, and support can lead you to become angry and resentful (both at yourself as well as at others). Being naturally hypersensitive to tension, you avoid conflict and can easily dissociate via mind, body, or spirit.

### Prescriptions for Stress

☞ Work with affirmations (using cards, tapes, books, or a coach) for continued healthy self-esteem and to maintain clear identity boundaries.

☞ Try inner work (interactive imagery, guided visualization, centering prayer, etc.) for "time-in" and realignment and integrating yourself.

☞ Practice creative expression in any preferred modes—painting, music, crafting, baking, writing, etc.

☞ Learn to identify, set and respect healthy limits and boundaries for yourself and others via books, tapes, classes, etc.

## How You Learn

Your most rewarding learning experiences include opportunities to communicate and share values, and to help yourself and others succeed in relationships. You seek learning opportunities where you can grow and that help you heed the call to a life work or mission. You enjoy the creative process and using your intuitive intellect to find ways to reconcile the past and the future. All of these help you see the potential in others, and you like learning more about how to help them achieve their potential. You love to learn how to help realize dreams—your own and others'.

## For Your Career Mastery

You will make plans and move decisively to make a career change or to find an environment that will support your need to meet new people and to make creative things happen. You will have a broad range of contacts and actively network with others. You may miss opportunities that come from turning inward to clarify what *you* need as distinct from what might benefit others. Your enthusiasm, communication skills, and willingness to be a team player are pluses. When connecting with others, you'll demonstrate your concern for people and that you are a quick learner, but be sure to communicate your task orientation as well as your people skills and to listen as well as talk in interviews. Don't let sensitivity to rejection get in the way of reaching out. You will naturally talk to others and need just a hint of an exciting possibility before making a decision. Resist the tendency to overlook key job facts in your desire to make a decision. You will weigh the impact of decisions on your personal life and significant others but may not look in a tough-minded way at the pros, and especially the cons, of any given option. You may weigh what others want too heavily. You are good at setting goals and following through. Remember that many good opportunities come through events that aren't planned.

### Challenge Yourself

Gather information and don't rush decisions. Pay attention to the facts/requirements of a job, look at the pros and cons of choices, and don't take tough search experiences personally.

## Reminders for Personal Growth

Maintain multiple sources of intuitive insight. It's okay to sense what others don't. Arrange your life and career so you get rewarded for your creative endeavors. Don't discard parts of yourself just to please someone else, nor should others have to discard parts of themselves to please you. If it feels like people are hurting you, then voice which of your values they are violating. Exercise and other physical activities are a great way to relax. Be more open to people's values—people sense if you like them or not. If your dreams guide your daily choices, then don't expect the fruits of a conventional life at the end of the rainbow. Remind yourself that your unconscious is in charge of your personal growth. Life has a way of unfolding according to its own design. If you want someone to change, really notice what they do to show they care. Consider that some people aren't rude, they're just different. Disillusionment leads to negativity and the misinterpretation of others' intent. Remember your power.

31

Temperament: **Catalyst™** · Interaction Style: **Chart-the-Course™** · Cognitive Processes: **Ni, Fe, Ti, Se | Ne, Fi, Te, Si**

## Snapshot

Theme is foresight. They use their insights to deal with complexity in issues and people, often with a strong sense of "knowing" before others know themselves. Their talents lie in developing and guiding people. They trust their inspirations and visions, using them to help others. They thrive on helping others resolve deep personal and ethical dilemmas. Private and complex, they bring a quiet enthusiasm and industry to projects that are part of their vision.

## When Solving Problems

Decisions are made quickly if the information matches their impressions and slowly if new information must be integrated into their understanding of the people system. They gather personal information, including global impressions, feelings, and emotional tone, comparing them to impressions and symbolic meaning. Decisions are most often based on impact on the people in the system. Inaction may result when they have no idea of the next step or they are overwhelmed with the physical realities of a situation. To influence them, show them another perspective and talk about the future and how a decision will affect others. Give them time to integrate new information into their vision and their models of how things will be.

## Style of Leadership

Their leadership style is characterized as individualistic with creative, idealistic, and insightful perspectives. They are masterful at facilitating an understanding of an organization's vision and gaining interpersonal commitments toward fulfillment of that vision. Their zeal for any given leadership situation is related to the core values embedded in their personal mission. Confident that their vision and mission is important, they will invest whatever energy is necessary to encourage, support, and organize efforts related to the vision. Often more concerned about the congruence of mission and values than with identifying concrete and realistic objectives, their strength, which is in building relationships of commitment toward a vision, may become a weakness if they are perceived as unrealistic about the challenges that must be met to actualize a plan.

## Creative Expression

Their creativity is realized in planning a route to accomplish a task that encourages developmental growth of the individuals engaged in the task's execution and those who are recipients of the end result. The plight of perfection hovers and motivates them to make a personally fulfilling change to help each to benefit from his or her role in the process. Time is spent incubating on ideas and visions of reaching the goal. They have a sense about what people need in order to grow and covertly match tasks to people who need to learn from doing them. This is the source of their creativity—making something out of potential, even if sweat work is involved, and gently persuading and affirming the accomplishments and gifts of others in meaningful ways.

## On a Team

### Naturally Bring to a Team

⇨ Have a talent for developing and guiding people; their relationships are about supporting human potential
⇨ Bring a quiet enthusiasm and industry to projects that are part of their vision
⇨ Organized, with a strong sense of purpose
⇨ Loyal to both people and organizations
⇨ Actively listen and give their full attention to others

### Teamwork Style

⇨ Lead quietly and by example in a predictable, orderly, and very personal way
⇨ Use insight and interpersonal warmth to organize, counsel, inspire, and teach
⇨ Inspire others with a positive, enthusiastic approach
⇨ Approach problems from a global perspective

### Potential Blind Spots

⇨ Can be seen as distant by others as they try to manage their own emotions
⇨ May lose sight of their own needs and personal identity, leading to eventual burnout
⇨ Might focus on developing people to such an extent that they lose a sense of perspective
⇨ May have difficulty separating their personal values from the impersonal

### To Help Them Succeed

⇨ Try to create an open, honest, and sincere relationship with them
⇨ Provide a work environment that focuses on people and their needs, with an identity and purpose that goes beyond everyday routine
⇨ Give them positive feedback

## Dealing with Your Stress

You experience stress when it appears to you that no one is listening to your foresights. You take your unique and intuitive abilities seriously and when others are inattentive and/or dismissive, you can experience significant degrees of tension and anxiety. In such situations, you perceive your very authenticity as being brought into question and cast in doubt. With a keen focus on possibilities coupled with trusting your intuitions, you can become deeply disillusioned whenever an organizational environment doesn't support your vision (and hence your role within it). When your image of "what I knowingly can and ought to be doing here" is blocked or derailed, you can become edgy and worrisome and begin fueling your fears. To say, "If I can't be who I know I can be here, then I'll have to be someone I'm not to fit in and match the system" can lead to a constant sense of pressure and become a severe energy drain.

### Prescriptions for Stress

☞ "Time-in" practices—journaling, creative writing, listening to and/or playing music, meditation, creative visualization work, guided imagery—are always good medicine.

☞ A sure destressor/decompressor is connecting with nature in some fashion on a regular basis. Anything from camping, trail walking, bird watching, star gazing, beach-combing, or a simple bicycle ride in the park has benefit.

☞ Constant refueling via creative expression is a "must do" for any wellness program you may design for yourself. The healthy focus is on "honoring your muse."

☞ Explore helpful options that are open to getting assistance with the business side of creative projects and/or chosen career paths.

## How You Learn

You find learning most rewarding when it is focused on personal growth and sustaining a vision. You like the type of learning that helps others explore issues and bridge differences, as well as learning that connects people. You really want your learning to help you live your idealistic life, so it must include practical problem solving to be really valuable. You honor the gifts of others and love to learn what you can do to help them develop those gifts. If what you are learning helps you take a creative approach to life and live with a greater sense of purpose, so much the better.

## For Your Career Mastery

You will quietly consider a number of ideal long-term career options before taking action and will seek environments that meet your needs to be imaginative, focused, and to help others. You will connect with a focal group of contacts but may miss opportunities that come from larger-scale efforts to connect with others who might have helpful information or valuable contacts. Your interpersonal skills, insight, and ability to be a quick learner are pluses. When connecting with others, be sure to sell yourself, your task orientation, and your ability to have practical impact, in addition to your people skills. Feelings that the job search is grueling or that you cannot find your ideal position may get in the way of taking action. You will naturally gather information through reading and get excited about a new career idea but may not register key facts and details about a career option. You will weigh the impact of decisions on yourself and significant others but may not look in a tough-minded way at the pros, and especially the cons, of any given option. You may weigh what others want too heavily. You are good at setting goals but may need to narrow the focus on exciting possibilities to an explorable short list so practical action can be taken.

### Challenge Yourself

Reach out to others, sell yourself, tentatively narrow your options so you can really move into action and gather facts/data about your options.

## Reminders for Personal Growth

Find an arena where your foresight is valued. Allow time to enjoy talking for fun with people whose interests and visions lie in the future. Own your ability to reframe a situation or interaction as one of your greatest gifts. To live in the moment, remember to share what you and others are hearing, seeing, and feeling right now. Have a safety net (time and space) to retreat to when overwhelmed by stress and the physical world. Remember that theories are nice tools to further exploration. If your understanding of something doesn't suggest how change or growth is possible, then add more depth and experience to that understanding. Balance what is supportive, friendly, and safe with what challenges the thinking behind your opinions. Have outlets to express life's many layers and levels. Try to imagine sometimes that you are like everyone else. After a period of personal growth, check for external evidence of change. Keep in mind that learning *how* to think is more useful than *what* to think.

33

Discoverer Advocate™

Temperament: **Catalyst**™ · Interaction Style: **Get-Things-Going**™ · Cognitive Processes: **Ne, Fi, Te, Si | Ni, Fe, Ti, Se**

## Snapshot

Theme is inspiration, both of themselves and others. Their talents lie in grasping profound significance, revealing truths, and motivating others. Very perceptive of others' hidden motives and purposes, they are interested in everything about individuals and their stories as long as they are genuine. They have a contagious enthusiasm for "causes" that further good and develop latent potential and have the same zeal for revealing dishonesty and inauthenticity. Frequently, they are moved to enthusiastically communicate their "message."

## When Solving Problems

They make quick decisions in response to opportunities that match the "ideal," or may deliberate over choosing the one right thing. They can get overwhelmed by all the options they see if they are not thoroughly in touch with their values. They generate possibilities based on the global impressions, feelings, and emotional tones they read in a situation. They respond to their immediate impressions and will either take action accordingly or put off deciding if personal values are not evoked. Decisions are based on what is individually and universally important. To influence them, show them another perspective or option that will be good for people and does not go against their values.

## Style of Leadership

Their leadership style is characterized by imaginative use of ideas and an enthusiastic rallying of the troops to achieve stated objectives. Expressive and cooperative, they tend to be adaptable and collaborative when working with others. They actively engage people in democratic decision making and in efforts related to their values of promoting growth and well-being. Innovative problem solvers, their approach to situations as leaders is to find the "basic good" in those involved and promote a new pathway toward a solution. Masterful at making connections between events, people, and situations, they communicate insights quickly and passionately. More concerned with their ideals and relationships with people than the structures or procedures needed to execute given tasks, their strength, when overdone, can derail them if they fail to focus on the important details needed to implement a plan.

## Creative Expression

Their creativity engages the promise for people to grow beyond themselves in sparkling and inspiring ways. Their energy percolates potentials for what is truly important to each individual, including themselves. Motivated to work with others to achieve a synergistic result, they are committed to the ideal that contributions of the group hold more promise than the voice of any one individual. Everyone must contribute. Their hope for the future leads when they speak. Moving forward is important, not standing still. Collaborating with others is a must. Their creativity is realized in working with others and using metaphoric thinking with verbal liveliness in a playfully divergent environment.

## On a Team

### Naturally Bring to a Team

⇨ A talent for grasping profound significance, revealing truths, and motivating others; their relationships are about getting involved at a personal, empathic level
⇨ Tend to be great at people skills—listening, facilitating, training, motivating, recruiting, counseling, and understanding others' perspectives
⇨ Keep communication channels open to make the best of a situation
⇨ An understanding of others that fosters collaborative teamwork and yet encourages individual contributions to the team

### Teamwork Style

⇨ Are highly people oriented, they lead with their energy and enthusiasm for causes
⇨ Get involved with individuals on a personal level, inspiring and facilitating them to find and reach their full potential
⇨ Focus on other's concerns, listen and negotiate when differences threaten the team

### Potential Blind Spots

⇨ May make strong assumptions and projections that are incorrect
⇨ Can easily get bored with routine, becoming depressed and failing to carry out ongoing projects to completion
⇨ Might focus so much on interpersonal issues in a situation that they forget the task and pull the team off track
⇨ May be seen as too talkative or as randomly interjecting ideas

### To Help Them Succeed

⇨ Provide a warm, understanding, and people-oriented work environment
⇨ Provide minimal insistence on rules, systems and procedures (mechanical restrictions)
⇨ Honor their need to authentically live with themselves
⇨ Help them recognize that what is easy to conceive often takes longer to achieve

Discoverer Advocate™ | **Being an ENFP**

Temperament: **Catalyst™** · Interaction Style: **Get-Things-Going™** · Cognitive Processes: **Ne, Fi, Te, Si | Ni, Fe, Ti, Se**

## Dealing with Your Stress

You find it stressful to be in an organization where there is nothing to advocate for. Being in a context where people don't want to "evolve" or discover truths and untruths about self and others leaves you uninspired as well as irritated. Being highly energetic and creative, with a natural bent to support system-wide growth and betterment, you are frustrated when such a posture is resisted or even denounced. Being overly energetic, you must have healthy outlets for channeling and expending your energies to avoid feeling "dammed up." You are unfulfilled when not provided with a variety of opportunities to interact and get things and people moving. Predictably, you can spread yourself so thin that you begin to feel like you're "tearing" or coming apart. This experience can often manifest itself into a whirlwind of confusion. You are stressed and impatient with the finer (mundane) details of projects, operational procedures, and people's insistence on taking time to discuss them.

### Prescriptions for Stress

☞ Use any and all forms of relaxation training and breathwork, invaluable antidotes for your particular stress. Whether through books, tapes, or private instruction, such practices done on a daily basis are the foundation for building a wellness program.

☞ Learn to set healthy, realistic limits—for self and others—in line with personal goals and aspirations.

☞ Review and update assertive behavior skills with books, classes, and so on.

☞ Set up an exercise/physical fitness program that includes a fair degree of physical exertion and "muscle work."

☞ Entertain established friends and family.

## How You Learn

Your most meaningful learning is inspiring and helps you facilitate others. If your learning provides you with what you need to authentically live with yourself, then you can learn anything. You need an opportunity to respond to insights in the creative process. Recognizing happiness, living out stories, and finding the magical situation motivate you to learn. You love exploring perceptions, seeing what's not being said, and voicing unspoken meanings. Sometimes this talent of yours can interfere with your learning if too much is going on beneath the surface, getting in the way of relationships.

## For Your Career Mastery

You will move quickly and spontaneously on career options if an exciting new possibility arises or if there is an opportunity to meet new people and to be innovative. You will actively network with a wide variety of people to explore options. You may miss opportunities that come from turning inward to examine the long-term direction of your career. Your energy, ingenuity, people skills, and versatility are pluses. When connecting with others, you will sell yourself with confidence and come across as a team player, but be sure to communicate your serious side and your task skills and to let others talk during interviews. You will get excited when talking to others about new career ideas but may fail to register key facts about career options. Resist the urge to be distracted by interesting side pursuits during the planning and search. You will weigh impact of decisions on personal life and significant others but may not look in a tough-minded way at the pros, and especially the cons, of any given option. You may need to narrow the possibilities to an explorable short list so action can be taken—otherwise action and decision making may be postponed indefinitely. You are responsive to unplanned opportunities but may not have worked out a long-term direction.

### Challenge Yourself

Develop long-term career goals, tentatively narrow your options so you can take concrete action, and gather facts about job options. Set deadlines for making decisions, decide, and follow through.

## Reminders for Personal Growth

Find and stay with what creates inspiring moments for you. Give people you encounter a second evaluation—to perceive what you missed the first time. Keep up with friends. It's okay to need inspiration for yourself. Check your perceptions of others. In a conflict, talk about yourself too. Have a work environment where you can be involved in numerous projects and flow creatively. Find times to let up on the need for constant change. Words are only words, so be honest about whether actions match intentions. Don't let who you think you are get in the way of who you can be. A good direction in life is to make something totally novel a new tradition. Trust that you can safely be yourself when people get close. Be sure you like who you're with. Practice patience with those who complain but do nothing about it. In any situation, try to always recognize at least three interpretations grounded in common sense. Good empathic connections require compassion. Consider that thinking everything is in the mind may just be wishful thinking.

35

## Understanding the INFP — Harmonizer Clarifier™

Temperament: **Catalyst™** · Interaction Style: **Behind-the-Scenes™** · Cognitive Processes: **Fi, Ne, Si, Te | Fe, Ni, Se, Ti**

## Snapshot

Theme is advocacy and integrity. Their talents lie in helping people clarify issues, values, and identity. They support anything that allows the unfolding of the person. They encourage growth and development with quiet enthusiasm. Loyal advocates and champions, they care deeply about their causes and a few special people. They are interested in contemplating life's mysteries, virtues, and vices in their search for wholeness. They thrive on healing conflicts, within and between, and taking people to the center of themselves.

## When Solving Problems

They quickly decide if something or someone is congruent yet decide slowly regarding actions to take. They are generally quite aware of implications and meanings of different actions, so they may vacillate until they are sure values are not violated. They gather personal information, including global impressions and feeling-tones. Inaction may result if personal values conflict with external demands for action and many differing values have to be reconciled and unified in one decision. They tend to take in a lot of information and play with a lot of ideas yet may act on impulse once values are aligned. To influence them, show them how new options are congruent with deep values.

## Style of Leadership

Their leadership style is characterized as passionate about causes, values, and ideals. Quite engaged with the generation of possibilities related to actualizing their mission, they try to motivate through encouraging others to reach their potential. While they enjoy working independently as it allows focus and concentration, they work effectively with small groups who are engaged in activities related to or reflective of values they hold most dear. More concerned with empathetic understanding than with immediate results, their natural strength of perceiving and acting on intuitions about others' needs may become a weakness if they seem unable to make tough decisions or confront problem associates and direct reports, thus seeming to create inefficiencies and lower productivity.

## Creative Expression

Their creativity is activated when opportunities to move forward on a personal dream of peace, truth, and beauty are encountered. Self-expression is engaged, at times in collaboration with others, to focus on what is right and to correct a perceived wrong. Any action that has a negative impact on a person's sense of self-esteem, value, and worth may serve as a trigger. Events, people, and philosophies mystify them. Time is spent musing on how each symbolically aligns with his or her staunch commitment to an inner ideal of helping oneself and others to grow in awareness of all there is. As ethicists, they monitor actions and decisions that demonstrate the values of individuals, teams, and organizations.

## On a Team

### Naturally Bring to a Team

⇨ A talent for facilitative listening and knowing what is behind what is said; their relationships are about helping people clarify issues, values, and identity
⇨ Identify strongly with others, appearing to know just what the other person needs to function better
⇨ Great people skills—listening, facilitating, motivating, recruiting, counseling
⇨ Create unity and harmony within a team by listening with empathy

### Teamwork Style

⇨ People oriented, they participate by quietly championing worthwhile causes and encouraging individuals to achieve
⇨ Supportive, caring, democratic, and participative, they foster growth and development through the affirmation of individual members
⇨ Have minimal focus on rules and procedures that are seen to inhibit freedom and autonomy

### Potential Blind Spots

⇨ May become so absorbed in a project that they can lose sight of what is taking place around them and appear to be unfocused
⇨ Might concentrate on deeper issues and can lose a sense of perspective
⇨ Can have difficulty with structure
⇨ May become overzealous about a value and find it difficult to acknowledge another's point of view

### To Help Them Succeed

⇨ Provide a sense of integrity and opportunities for fostering wholeness, harmony, and mental health in others
⇨ Give them the flexibility to capitalize on bursts of energy and not be berated for the lulls in between
⇨ Let them work alone when they need to; interacting with a great number of people at once may drain their energy
⇨ Help them to find personal meaning in a project

Temperament: **Catalyst™** · Interaction Style: **Behind-the-Scenes™** · Cognitive Processes: **Fi, Ne, Si, Te | Fe, Ni, Se, Ti**

## Dealing with Your Stress

Being a natural harmonizer and talented at getting everyone in sync, your behavior can take on the air/look of a noble cause or purpose, leading to your energies being rapidly and easily depleted. Although your preferred method is that of "quietly" informing and clarifying, the stress of not getting heard can lead to "loudly" insisting, demanding and criticizing. Your constant seeking of unity and wholeness can paradoxically result in your losing who you are—especially when it's not safe to be who you are within an organization. Indeed, as a coping/survival reaction to chronic stress, you take on the whole persona of the work you need to do i.e., looking like the personality of the job. All the while the inner self is saying, with frustration and fear, "This isn't really me." A staunch defender of your values and belief system and the quintessential "idealist," you are easily disheartened and unsettled by the realities of the mainstream and painfully aware of how you don't often fit in.

### Prescriptions for Stress

☞ Constantly review and reset personal goals and objectives for self.

☞ Develop the ability to set healthy boundaries through classes, books, tapes, or through one-on-one coaching/counseling.

☞ Establish a relationship with someone who is an empathic listener.

☞ Use any activities, techniques, or exercises that function as sources of "refueling." Whether engaged solo or with significant others, such daily re-energizing practices ought to be part of a healthy lifestyle.

## How You Learn

You learn best when you can just "go with the flow." You like uncovering mysteries and exploring moral questions. You relate through stories and metaphors that help you balance the many opposing forces of life. You have a way of knowing what is behind what is said, so sometimes that is what grabs your attention. You use your talent for facilitative listening to really learn, especially about yourself and others. Learning that helps you get reacquainted with yourself is the most rewarding. You have a way of knowing what is believable and will judge your learning experience by that.

## For Your Career Mastery

You will quietly reflect on how well the current environment fits with personal ideals while considering other long-term options that might meet your need to make valuable contributions to people and to be creative. You will connect with a focal group of contacts but may miss opportunities that come from larger-scale efforts to connect with others who might have helpful information or valuable contacts. Your communication skills, creativity, and ability to be a quick learner are pluses. When connecting with others, be sure to sell your strong points and to communicate your task orientation in addition to your people and language skills. Don't let waiting for the perfect job or lack of confidence in your abilities get in the way of taking action. You will naturally gather information through reading and self-exploration but may not register key facts about a career option. You will weigh the impact of decisions on yourself and significant others but may not look in a tough-minded way at the pros, and especially the cons, of any given option. You may weigh what others want too heavily. You may need to narrow the possibilities to an explorable short list so action can be taken—otherwise action and decision making may be postponed indefinitely.

### Challenge Yourself

Reach out to others, sell your strengths and accomplishments, narrow your options down so you can take concrete action, gather facts about job options, and follow through on your career search plan.

## Reminders for Personal Growth

Connect with people who create the kind of organization where you can be empathic. Try to stay tuned in to alternate beliefs. Pay some attention to your health and physical environment—it's not as scary as you imagine. Try to gather three facts about important situations, even if you must ask. With a project, try to do a little work every day. When something seems unbelievable, consider what is really an aspect of your identity and what is simply a hasty evaluation about its worth. If you can't "be there" emotionally for a person, then introduce them to someone who can. Realize that your words may cause people to reconsider who they are and what they believe in. Good reasoning involves considering multiple counter-arguments. Ground your beliefs in the lives of many real people. If you're going to use an idea ethically, then seriously learn the specifics. Don't get seduced by the "dark side" or a reactionary identity. It's okay to imagine "as if" you had a certain plan. If you wait to hear what sounds good, consider how you can work out the negative feelings.

37

## MTR-i™ Team Roles

An MTR-i™ Team Role results from the use of a cognitive process. Usage of cognitive processes is different from preference. This can be illustrated using the following well-known exercise: Write your name with your preferred hand; then write it with your other hand. Your preference is always for the same hand, but you use one hand and then the other.

In the same way, your preferences for certain cognitive processes remain the same, as may be indicated by personality type instruments. However, different situations may require the use of different cognitive processes, as may be indicated by the MTR-i™ questionnaire.

Where there is a difference between your preference and usage, this indicates a "stretch." If your stretch is too big, it can cause stress. If it is too small, it can result in stagnation.

| Personality Type Instruments | MTR-i™ |
|---|---|
| • Report personality type | • Reports contribution to the team |
| • Consistent over time | • Changes in different situations |
| • Measure preferences for cognitive processes | • Measures usage of cognitive processes |
| • Report 4 pairs of preferences resulting in 16 personality types | • Reports 8 distinct team roles |

## The Eight MTR-i™ Team Roles

38

### Coach, extraverted Feeling—Fe

Coaches try to create harmony in the world around them by building rapport with people, creating a positive team atmosphere, looking after people's welfare, motivating people, and/or providing a service to the satisfaction of others. They value people's contributions, seek to develop the role that others play, and invest a lot of effort in building positive relationships. They try to overcome differences of opinion and find ways in which the team can agree.

### Campaigner, introverted Feeling—Fi

Campaigners give importance to particular thoughts, ideas, or beliefs. They are value driven, and in a team discussion they often bring a sense of priority that is derived from their strong convictions. They seize upon and emphasize ideas or thoughts that have the greatest import, bringing them to the fore and stressing their significance. They assess the inherent value or importance of new ideas, focusing on those about which they feel most strongly.

### Explorer, extraverted iNtuiting—Ne

Explorers promote exploration of new and better ways of doing things, to uncover hidden potential in people, things, or situations. They break new ground and are often looking one step beyond the current situation to pursue unexplored avenues until all the possibilities have been exhausted. Explorers often challenge the status quo and experiment with the introduction of change to see if a situation can be improved or new potential uncovered.

### Innovator, introverted iNtuiting—Ni

Innovators use their imagination to create new and different ideas and perspectives. They observe the world around them then use their imaginations to consider what they have observed from a number of different perspectives and dream up new ideas and insights. Innovators often produce radical solutions to problems, develop long-term vision, and demonstrate an apparent understanding of what cannot be clearly known.

### Sculptor, extraverted Sensing—Se

Sculptors bring things to fruition by getting things done, and getting them done now! They are very action-oriented, dealing with whatever tasks the current situation presents, and spurring others into action as well. They make use of their experience and utilize tools or processes of which they already have knowledge. They try to have an immediate impact on things, injecting a sense of urgency and aiming to achieve clear goals and tangible results.

### Curator, introverted Sensing—Si

Curators bring clarity to the inner world of information, ideas, and understanding. They listen, ask questions, and absorb information so that in their mind's eye they can achieve as clear a picture or understanding as is possible. They expand their knowledge and collection of experiences and also look to the future by envisaging clear goals and clear pathways to achievement of those goals. The focus on clarity also brings greater attention to detail.

## Conductor, extraverted Thinking—Te

Conductors introduce organization and a logical structure into the way things are done. They organize and systematize the world around them, establishing appropriate plans, identifying and implementing the correct procedures, and then endeavoring to make sure they are followed. They try to ensure that roles and responsibilities are properly defined and that appropriate resources or skills are available to undertake the work assigned.

## Scientist, introverted Thinking—Ti

Scientists provide explanations of how and why things happen. They bring structure and organization into the inner world of ideas and understanding. They analyze things, formulating hypotheses and explanations of how they function, and gather evidence to assess how true those explanations are. They produce mental models that replicate how particular aspects of the world work, and they try to understand the full complexity of any situation.

## The 16 Personality Types and the MTR-i™ Team Roles

| | | | |
|---|---|---|---|
| **ISTJ** | **ISFJ** | **INFJ** | **INTJ** |
| ISTJ can undertake any team role but often prefer Curator first, then Conductor, and then Scientist. They often prefer Explorer and Coach least. | ISFJ can undertake any team role but often prefer Curator first, then Coach, and then Campaigner. They often prefer Explorer and Conductor least. | INFJ can undertake any team role but often prefer Innovator first, then Coach, and then Campaigner. They often prefer Sculptor and Conductor least. | INTJ can undertake any team role but often prefer Innovator first, then Conductor, and then Scientist. They often prefer Sculptor and Coach least. |
| **Curator** | **Curator** | **Innovator** | **Innovator** |
| **ISTP** | **ISFP** | **INFP** | **INTP** |
| ISTP can undertake any team role but often prefer Scientist first, then Sculptor, and then Curator. They often prefer Coach and Explorer least. | ISFP can undertake any team role but often prefer Campaigner first, then Sculptor, and then Curator. They often prefer Conductor and Explorer least. | INFP can undertake any team role but often prefer Campaigner first, then Explorer, and then Innovator. They often prefer Conductor and Sculptor least. | INTP can undertake any team role, but often prefer Scientist first, then Explorer, and then Innovator. They often prefer Coach and Sculptor least. |
| **Scientist** | **Campaigner** | **Campaigner** | **Scientist** |
| **ESTP** | **ESFP** | **ENFP** | **ENTP** |
| ESTP can undertake any team role but often prefer Sculptor first, then Scientist, and then Conductor. They often prefer Innovator and Campaigner least. | ESFP can undertake any team role but often prefer Sculptor first, then Campaigner, and then Coach. They often prefer Innovator and Scientist least. | ENFP can undertake any team role but often prefer Explorer first, then Campaigner, and then Coach. They often prefer Curator and Scientist least. | ENTP can undertake any team role but often prefer Explorer first, then Scientist, and then Conductor. They often prefer Curator and Campaigner least. |
| **Sculptor** | **Sculptor** | **Explorer** | **Explorer** |
| **ESTJ** | **ESFJ** | **ENFJ** | **ENTJ** |
| ESTJ can undertake any team role but often prefer Conductor first, then Curator, and then Sculptor. They often prefer Campaigner and Innovator least. | ESFJ can undertake any team role but often prefer Coach first, then Curator, and then Sculptor. They often prefer Scientist and Innovator least. | ENFJ can undertake any team role but often prefer Coach first, then Innovator, and then Explorer. They often prefer Scientist and Curator least. | ENTJ can undertake any team role but often prefer Conductor first, then Innovator, and then Explorer. They often prefer Campaigner and Curator least. |
| **Conductor** | **Coach** | **Coach** | **Conductor** |

*NOTE: The MTR-i™ Team Roles are organized within "The Type Table." See Appendix B: Organizing the 16 Types for more information.*

39

## Displaying the 16 Personality Types

Different practitioners and different publications use various ways of displaying the types to show their similarities and differences. Each of these ways of organizing puts the focus on a different aspect of understanding the sixteen types and has different uses.

## Type Table

The Type Table was created by Isabel Myers to display the types together that have the most in common. It is organized around the two middle letters in the type code called "functional pairs." These two letters refer to the preferred mode of perception and the preferred mode of judgment for that type pattern. Using Myers' interpretation of Jung, the focus is on the columns of the type table and many type practitioners group people by functional pair in activities that highlight differences and points of conflict. Myers also wanted to put the two types that share a preference for the same dominant function in

the same attitude next to each other. For example, ISTJ and ISFJ both have dominant introverted Sensing (Si) and are side by side. Her system works if you think of the table as a cylinder that puts INTP and ISTP side by side and ENTJ and ESTJ side by side.

The left side of the table displays the types with a Sensing preference and the right side displays those with a preference for iNtuiting (iNtuition). The top half consists of the eight types which are introverted and the bottom half, those which are extraverted. The top and bottom row are the types with a Judging preference and the two middle rows are the types with a Perceiving preference for dealing with the outer world. The outside columns display the types with a Thinking preference and the middle columns display those with a Feeling preference.

The type table is the standard way of reporting type related research and those who focus on Jung's theory of psychological types find this way of displaying the sixteen types the most useful for referring to that theory. (See appendix A for an application of this.)

### The Type Table

|  |  | SENSING | | INTUITION | |
| --- | --- | --- | --- | --- | --- |
|  |  | THINKING | FEELING | FEELING | THINKING |
| INTROVERSION | JUDGEMENT | **ISTJ**<br>Dominant:<br>**Introverted Sensing—Si**<br>Auxiliary:<br>**Extraverted Thinking—Te** | **ISFJ**<br>Dominant:<br>**Introverted Sensing—Si**<br>Auxiliary:<br>**Extraverted Feeling—Fe** | **INFJ**<br>Dominant:<br>**Introverted iNtuiting—Ni**<br>Auxiliary:<br>**Extraverted Feeling—Fe** | **INTJ**<br>Dominant:<br>**Introverted iNtuiting—Ni**<br>Auxiliary:<br>**Extraverted Thinking—Te** |
| INTROVERSION | PERCEPTION | **ISTP**<br>Dominant:<br>**Introverted Thinking—Ti**<br>Auxiliary:<br>**Extraverted Sensing—Se** | **ISFP**<br>Dominant:<br>**Introverted Feeling—Fi**<br>Auxiliary:<br>**Extraverted Sensing—Se** | **INFP**<br>Dominant:<br>**Introverted Feeling—Fi**<br>Auxiliary:<br>**Extraverted iNtuiting—Ne** | **INTP**<br>Dominant:<br>**Introverted Thinking—Ti**<br>Auxiliary:<br>**Extraverted iNtuiting—Ne** |
| EXTRAVERSION | PERCEPTION | **ESTP**<br>Dominant:<br>**Extraverted Sensing—Se**<br>Auxiliary:<br>**Introverted Thinking—Ti** | **ESFP**<br>Dominant:<br>**Extraverted Sensing—Se**<br>Auxiliary:<br>**Introverted Feeling—Fi** | **ENFP**<br>Dominant:<br>**Extraverted iNtuiting—Ne**<br>Auxiliary:<br>**Introverted Feeling—Fi** | **ENTP**<br>Dominant:<br>**Extraverted iNtuiting—Ne**<br>Auxiliary:<br>**Introverted Thinking—Ti** |
| EXTRAVERSION | JUDGEMENT | **ESTJ**<br>Dominant:<br>**Extraverted Thinking—Te**<br>Auxiliary:<br>**Introverted Sensing—Si** | **ESFJ**<br>Dominant:<br>**Extraverted Feeling—Fe**<br>Auxiliary:<br>**Introverted Sensing—Si** | **ENFJ**<br>Dominant:<br>**Extraverted Feeling—Fe**<br>Auxiliary:<br>**Introverted iNtuiting—Ni** | **ENTJ**<br>Dominant:<br>**Extraverted Thinking—Te**<br>Auxiliary:<br>**Introverted iNtuiting—Ni** |

40

## The Temperament Matrix™

The Temperament Matrix™ displays the Catalyst™ temperament (the types with N and F in their codes) and the Stabilizer™ Temperament (those with S and J in their type codes) on the top of the matrix to show that these two temperaments have a social attitude in common—they tend to take more affiliative roles and focus on interdependence. The Theorist™ temperament (with N and T in their codes) and the Improviser™ temperament (with S and P in their codes) are on the bottom of the matrix to show that they take on more pragmatic roles and focus on autonomy and independence. On the left are the two temperaments that tend to use abstract language and on the right are the two that tend to use concrete language. Since temperament theory is based in the Gestalt-Field-Systems school of thought, the focus is on thematic wholes rather than juxtaposition of traits.

Within each of the temperament cells in the matrix are placed the four Interaction Styles (Berens, 2001). These four styles occur within each temperament pattern and are "governed" or influenced by the primary motivation of the temperament pattern. This gets us to sixteen type patterns which behaviorally match the sixteen type patterns arrived at through Isabel Myers' interpretation of Jung. The rows and columns of the matrix do have commonalities. The left column shows the directing, abstract communicating types and the next column, the informing, abstract communicating types. The third column shows the directing, concrete communicating types and the last column, the informing concrete communicating types. The top and third rows show the responding varieties of that temperament and the second row shows the initiating varieties.

People who use temperament in their understanding of the types find the temperament matrix communicates a lot to them very quickly and they can see how each type has something in common with every other type as well as how they are different.

*NOTE*: Linda Berens introduced new terms for the 4 temperaments in *Understanding Yourself and Others®: An Introduction to the 4 Temepraments—3.0* (Telos Publications, 2006).

41

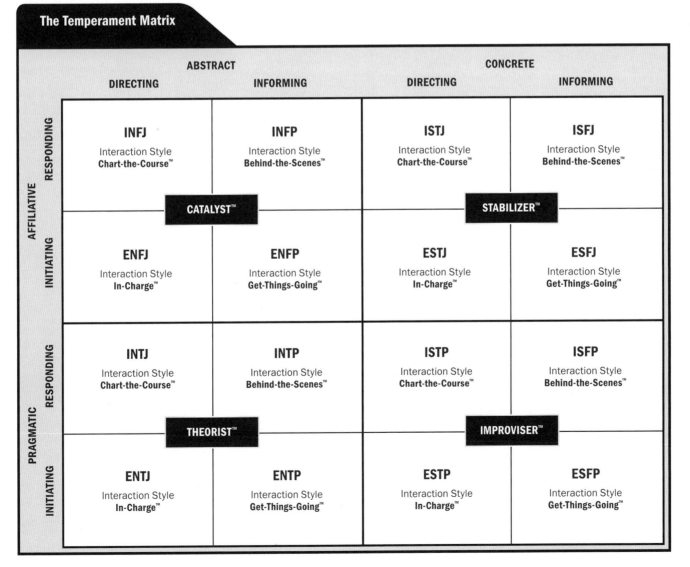

## Linda V. Berens, Ph.D.

Linda V. Berens is the director and founder of Interstrength® Associates (ISA), which provides organizational consulting and interventions as well as certification of trainers in The Interstrength® Method. She has qualified hundreds of professionals to administer and interpret the Myers-Briggs Type Indicator® (MBTI®) instrument, the most widely used personality instrument in the world. She is an organizational consultant and has spent over twenty-five years helping individuals and teams recognize their strengths, transcend their weaknesses, and work together better. Linda is recognized internationally for her theoretical contributions to the field of psychological type and for developing user-friendly training materials for practical application of understanding individual differences.

### Other titles by Linda V. Berens:

- *The 16 Personality Types: Descriptions for Self-Discovery* (1999)

- *Understanding Yourself and Others®: An Introduction to Interaction Styles* (2001)

- *Quick Guide to Interaction Styles and Working Remotely: Strategies for Leading and Working in Virtual Teams* (2003)

- *Quick Guide to the 16 Personality Types and Teams: Applying Team Essentials to Create Effective Teams* (2004)

- *Understanding Yourself and Others®: An Introduction to the Personality Type Code* (2004)

- *The I in TEAM: Accelerating Performance in Remote and Co-located Teams* (2005)

- *Understanding Yourself and Others®: An Introduction to the 4 Temperaments—3.0* (2006)

- *The Communication Zone™* (forthcoming)

## Sue A. Cooper, Ph.D., M.F.T.

Sue A. Cooper is a psychotherapist, educator, and certified Interactive Guided Imagery practitioner. She is considered an authority in the fields of intra- and inter-personal communication strategies, stress relief, temperament theory, and wellness programs. Sue has presented workshops on positive, results-oriented mental health practices for over twenty years. Her programs consist of a repertoire of tools presented to empower individuals to effect change. Currently Sue is involved in several writing projects and lives, plays, and works in Orange County, California, and beyond.

## Linda K. Ernst, M.S.

Linda Ernst is a trainer and consultant and president of Training Resource, an independently owned contract training service. Since 1983, she has conducted hundreds of custom-designed in-house workshops for a wide range of industrial and organizational clients. She has experience designing and facilitating workshops using psychological type for personal development, management development, team building, and for trainers. Linda is a co-author of *The Guide for Facilitating The Self-Discovery Process™*. As an instructional design consultant, she has helped organizations develop courses in topics that include leadership development, quality improvement, and communication skills for managers; consulting skills for trainers; and using type dynamics to facilitate teams.

### Other titles by Linda K. Ernst:

- *Quick Guide to the 16 Personality Types and Teams: Applying Team Essentials to Create Effective Teams* (2004)

## Charles R. Martin, Ph.D.

Charles R. Martin is a licensed psychologist engaged in a full-time consulting and coaching practice. In his coaching and consulting work, Dr. Martin's emphasis is on promoting self-mastery and effective living and working through the development of personal and professional skills. He draws on his background to use a variety of models and assessment tools to support clients in reaching their personal, professional, and organizational goals. He is a past vice president of research and development for the Center for Applications of Psychological Type (CAPT), and was the architect of CAPT's MBTI® Qualifying Program. Dr. Martin has trained and qualified hundreds of professionals to use personality type as a tool for both personal and professional development.

### Other titles by Charles R. Martin:

- *Looking at Type: The Fundamentals* (1995)

- *Looking at Type and Careers* (1996)

- *Building People, Building Programs: A Practitioner's Guide to Introducing the MBTI to Individuals and Organizations* (2001)

- *Quick Guide to the 16 Personality Types and Career Mastery: Living with Purpose and Working Effectively* (2002)

- *Out-of-the-Box Exercises: Using the Power of Type to Build Effective Teams* (2003)

## Steve Myers, B.S.

Steve Myers is the managing partner of Team Technology in the United Kingdom, an organization that specializes in team development. Steve works with type not only in running MBTI workshops, but also in undertaking type-related research and development, primarily using Internet-based questionnaires. From 1996 to 2000, he devised a method for measuring usage of the eight cognitive

42

processes in a study that involved over 20,000 participants and culminated in the publication of the Management Team Role-indicator™ (MTR-i™).

### Other titles by Steve Myers:

- *Influencing People Using Myers Briggs* (1995)
- *Management Team Role-indicator Manual* (2001)

## Dario Nardi, Ph.D.

Dario Nardi is currently an adjunct assistant professor of mathematics at the University of California, Los Angeles, in the department's Program in Computing. He has been working with type and temperament since 1992, has been intimately involved in innovative product development with the Temperament Research Institute for nine years, and has authored several papers on type research with students. Dario received his degree in systems science from the State University of New York at Binghamton's Watson School of Engineering. His background in systems thinking, linguistics and artificial intelligence, undergraduate curriculum design, and writing has led him to breakthroughs using multiple methods and models for getting at the "true self," as well as for restructuring academic courses to suit all learning styles.

### Other titles by Dario Nardi:

- *The 16 Personality Types: Descriptions for Self-Discovery* (1999)
- *Character and Personality Type: Discovering Your Uniqueness for Career and Relationship Success* (2000)
- *Multiple Intelligences and Personality Type: Tools and Strategies for Developing Human Potential* (2001)
- *Understanding Yourself and Others®: An Introduction to the Personality Type Code* (2004)
- *8 Keys to Self-Leadership: from Awareness to Action* (2005)

## Roger R. Pearman, Ph.D.

Roger Pearman is the principal of Leadership Performance Systems, Inc. He is an internationally recognized consultant, trainer, speaker, and author. A former college professor, psychotherapist, and corporate vice president, Roger is a senior adjunct trainer, feedback coach, and adjunct research associate with the Center for Creative Leadership. For nearly twenty years, he has helped individuals and groups face the challenges of change, working extensively with executives and leaders in government, business, education, and nonprofit organizations across North America and Europe.

### Other titles by Roger R. Pearman:

- *I'm Not Crazy, I'm Just Not You: The Real Meaning of the Sixteen Personality Types* (1997)
- *Hard Wired Leadership: Unleashing Personality for the New Millennium Leader* (1998)
- *Enhancing Leadership Effectiveness* (2000)
- *Leadership Advantage* (2001)
- *Introduction to Type® and Emotional Intelligence* (2002)
- *YOU: Being More Effective in Your MBTI® Type* (2006)

## Marci Segal, M.S.

Marci Segal is president of CreativityLand, Inc., an international innovation and creativity consulting network in Toronto, Canada. She uses the principles of creative studies and personality type to help individuals and communities within organizations develop a "best work" environment. Her education includes undergraduate and graduate work at the International Center for Studies in Creativity at the State University of New York College at Buffalo. She is an active member of the Creative Education Foundation and is a senior faculty member at the Creative Problem Solving Institute in Buffalo, New York, and San Diego, California. Marci is recognized worldwide for the contributions she has made to the fields of creativity and psychological type by integrating the frameworks for targeted and successful applications.

### Other titles by Marci Segal:

- *Creativity and Personality Type: Tools for Understanding and Inspiring the Many Voices of Creativity* (2001)
- *Quick Guide to the Four Temperaments and Creativity: A Psychological Understanding of Innovation* (2002)

## Melissa A. Smith, M.B.A.

Melissa Smith is a consultant and trainer specializing in management and organization development. She has designed and delivered numerous skill and management development programs, coached executives to improve group process and personal skills, and assisted organizations in planning and implementing culture changes. A skilled professional development trainer, Ms. Smith has extensive experience designing and facilitating workshops using personality type. Her methodology, which is based on action-learning principles, is designed uniquely for the client and is tailored for a specific purpose and output. She co-authored *The Guide for Facilitating The Self-Discovery Process*™ and is a master trainer of trainers.

### Other titles by Melissa A. Smith:

- *Quick Guide to the 16 Personality Types and Teams: Applying Team Essentials to Create Effective Teams* (2004)

43

Baron, Renee. *What Type Am I?*. New York: Penguin Putnam, 1998.

Berens, Linda V. and Dario Nardi *The 16 Personality Types: Descriptions for Self-Discovery.* Fountain Valley, Calif.: Telos Publications, 1999.

Berens, Linda V., Linda K. Ernst, and Melissa A. Smith. *Quick Guide to the 16 Personality Types and Teams: Applying Team Essentials to Create Effective Teams.* Huntington Beach, Calif.: Telos Publications, 2004.

Berens, Linda V. *Understanding Yourself and Others®: An Introduction to the 4 Temperaments—3.0.* Fountain Valley, Calif.: Telos Publications, 2006.

Berens, Linda V. *Understanding Yourself and Others®: An Introduction to the Personality Type Code.* Fountain Valley, Calif.: Telos Publications, 2004.

Berens, Linda V. *Understanding Yourself and Others®: An Introduction to Interaction Styles.* Fountain Valley, Calif.: Telos Publications, 2001.

Campbell, Scott. *Quick Guide to the Four Temperaments and Peak Performance: How to Unlock Your Talents to Excel At Work.* Huntington Beach, Calif.: Telos Publications, 2003.

Cooper, Brad. *Quick Guide to the Four Temperaments and Sales: An Introduction to the Groundbreaking Sales™ Methods.* Fountain Valley, Calif.: Telos Publications, 2003.

Cooper, Brad. and Linda V. Berens. *Groundbreaking Sales® Skills: Portable Sales Techniques™ to Ensure Success.* Huntington Beach, Calif.: Telos Publications, 2004.

Delunas, Eve, *Survival Games Personalities Play.* Carmel, Calif.: Sunflower Ink, 1992.

Dossett, Mary. and Julia Mallory. *Results by Design: Survival Skills for Project Managers.* Huntington Beach, Calif.: Telos Publications, 2004.

Dunning, Donna. *Quick Guide to the Four Temperaments and Learning: Practical Tools and Strategies for Enhancing Learning Effectiveness.* Huntington Beach, Calif.: Telos Publications, 2003.

Dunning, Donna. *Quick Guide to the Four Temperaments and Change: Strategies for Navigating Workplace Change.* Huntington Beach, Calif.: Telos Publications, 2004.

Dunning, Donna. *What's Your Type of Career: Unlock the Secrets of Your Personality to Find Your Perfect Career Path.* Palo Alto, Calif.: Davies-Black Publishing, 2001.

Fairhurst, Alice M., and Lisa L. Fairhurst, *Effective Teaching, Effective Learning.* Palo Alto, Calif.: Consulting Psychologists Press, Inc., 1995.

Fields, Margaret U., and Jean Reid (Editors), *Shape Up Your Program!.* Gainesville, Florida.: Center for Applications of Psychological Type, 2001.

Haas, Leona, and Mark Hunziker. *Building Blocks of Personality Type: A Guide to Using the Eight-Process Model of Personality Type.* Huntington Beach, Calif.: Telos Publications, 2006.

Hartzler, Gary, and Margaret Hartzler. *Facets of Type: Activities to Develop the Type Preferences.* Huntington Beach, Calif.: Telos Publications, 2004.

Hartzler, Gary, and Margaret Hartzler. *Functions of Type: Activities to Develop the Eight Jungian Functions.* Huntington Beach, Calif.: Telos Publications, 2005.

Hirsh, Sandra Krebs, and Jane A.G. Kise. *Work It Out: Clues for Solving People Problems at Work.* Palo Alto, Calif.: Davies-Black Publishing, 1996.

Gerke, Susan K., and Linda V. Berens *The I in TEAM: Accelerating Performance in Remote and Co-located Teams.* Huntington Beach, Calif.: Telos Publications, 2005.

Gerke, Susan K. and Linda V. Berens *Quick Guide to Interaction Styles and Working Remotely: Strategies for Leading and Working in Virtual Teams.* Fountain Valley, Calif.: Telos Publications, 2003.

Kise, Jane A.G., David Stark and Sandra Krebs Hirsh. *LifeKeys: Discovering...Who You Are, Why You're Here, What You Do Best.* Minneapolis: Bethany House Publishers, 1996.

Martin, Charles R., and Gordon Lawrence, *Building People, Building Programs.* Gainesville, Florida.: Center for Applications of Psychological Type, 2001.

Martin, Charles R. *Looking at Type and Careers.* Gainesville, Florida.: Center for Applications of Psychological Type, 1995.

Martin, Charles R. *Looking at Type: The Fundamentals.* Gainesville, Florida.: Center for Applications of Psychological Type, 1997.

Martin, Charles R. *Quick Guide to the 16 Personality Types and Career Mastery: Living with Purpose and Working Effectively.* Fountain Valley, Calif.: Telos Publications, 2003.

Michel, Sarah. *Perfecting Connecting®: Learning to Speak the Language of Others.* Audio. Huntington Beach, Calif.: Telos Publications, 2003.

Michel, Sarah. *Perfecting Connecting®: A Personal Guide to Mastering Networking in the Workplace.* Huntington Beach, Calif.: Telos Publications, 2004.

Myers, Isabel and Peter Myers (Contributor), *Gifts Differing.* Palo Alto, Calif.: Consulting Psychologists Press, 1995.

Myers, Steve, *Management Team Role Indicator® Manual.* United Kingdom.: The Test Agency, 2001.

Nardi, Dario. *8 Keys to Self-Leadership: From Awareness to Action.* Fountain Valley, Calif.: Telos Publications, 2005.

Nardi, Dario. *Multiple Intelligences and Personality Type: Tools and Strategies for Developing Human Potential.* Fountain Valley, Calif.: Telos Publications, 2000.

Nardi, Dario. *Character and Personality Type: Discovering Your Uniqueness for Career and Relationship Success.* Fountain Valley, Calif.: Telos Publications, 1999.

Nash, Susan. *Turning Team Performance Inside Out.* Palo Alto, Calif.: Davies-Black Publishing, 2000.

Pearman, Roger R. *Enhancing Leadership Effectiveness Through Psychological Type.* Gainsville, Florida: Center for Applications of Psychological Type, 1999.

Pearman, Roger R. *Hard Wired Leadership : Unleashing the Power of Personality to Become a New Millennium Leader.* Palo Alto, Calif.: Davies-Black Publishing, 1997.

Pearman, Roger R., and Sarah C. Albritton, (Contributor). *I'm Not Crazy, I'm Just Not You : The Real Meaning of the 16 Personality Types.* Palo Alto, Calif.: Consulting Psychologists Press, 1997.

Pearman, Roger R. *Introduction to Type® and Emotional Intelligence.* Palo Alto, Calif.: Consulting Psychologists Press, 2002.

Quenk, Naomi. *In the Grip.* Palo Alto, Calif.: Consulting Psychologists Press, 1985.

Segal, Marci. *Creativity and Personality Type: Tools for Understanding and Inspiring the Many Voices of Creativity.* Fountain Valley, Calif.: Telos Publications, 2001.

Segal, Marci. *Quick Guide to the Four Temperaments and Creativity: A Psychological Understanding of Innovation.* Fountain Valley, Calif.: Telos Publications, 2003.

Sharp, Daryl. *Personality Type, Jung's Model of Typology.* Toronto, Canada: Inner City Books, 1987.

**On the Internet**

16types.com®: www.16types.com

4temperaments.com: www.4temperaments.com

Best-Fit Type: www.bestfittype.com

Cognitive Processes: www.cognitiveprocesses.com

Interaction Styles: www.interactionstyles.com

Not Just A Paycheck®: www.notjustapaycheck.com

Telos Publications: www.telospublications.com

44

# QUICK GUIDE *TO THE*
# 16 PERSONALITY TYPES
# *IN* ORGANIZATIONS

## Understanding Personality Differences in the Workplace

The *Quick Guide to the 16 Personality Types in Organizations* is written by leading experts in the theory of personality type and its applications. This booklet helps you develop your personal effectiveness within the workplace by providing two full pages of information about each of the sixteen personality types under the topics of Problem Solving, Leadership, Creativity, Teams, Stress, Learning, Career Mastery, and Personal Development. Also included is an appendix that will help you understand the eight MTR-i™ team roles.

The first page of each description includes information on understanding the specific personality type to help you shift perspectives to improve your relationships with others. The second page includes information on being that personality type to help you further your understanding of yourself. This format makes this booklet essential for employees in any organization who want to understand themselves better and work with others more effectively.

---

### ADVANCE PRAISE

"The *Quick Guide* is masterfully concise for workshop use, yet rich with information for in-depth applications of type."
—Jane A.G. Kise
coauthor, *Lifekeys: Discovering...Who You Are, Why You're Here, What You Do Best*

---

"An invaluable handbook for developing individuals, teams, and organizations that covers fresh, new territory in a compact format."
—Eve Delunas
  *Survival Games Personalities Play*

---

"Compact portrayals of each type are consolidated into a user-frie_____ g in or with organizations. The areas covered represent key components of organizational life ____ the characterizations are concise, they are comprehensive and reflect the richness of type diversity."
—Margaret U. Fields
contributing author, *Leadership, Type, and Culture: Perspectives from Across the Globe*

---

"A wonderful collection of diverse thought that form one the most complete set of descriptions of psychological type's expression in organizations that I have ever read. The perfect reference for those who do organizational consulting or individual coaching."
—Mark S. Majors
**President, True Type Testing**

---

"It is good to see a book with descriptions of the 16 types that draws from the knowledge and data of many leaders in type theory. I think people reading this book will be inspired to live up to the potentials described and gain some tips on how to grow in areas of potential weaknesses."
—Margaret Hartzler
coauthor, *Journey of Understanding: MBTI® Interpretation Using the Eight Jungian Functions*

---

"These type descriptions provide a comprehensive insight into how personality type manifests itself at work, whether in teams, leadership or career development. They will be an essential support to my work with organizations!"
—Susan Nash
author, *Turning Team Performance Inside Out: Team Types and Temperament for High-Impact Results*

---

"Excellent resource for organizations and teams written by leaders in the personality type community. Right on the mark with topics that are important in today's work environment."
—Leona Haas
author, *Jung's Mental Processes: Building Blocks of Type*

---

# Telos
PUBLICATIONS

ISBN 0-9712144-1-7

www.telospublications.com